\

the way
of the
kabbalist

© 2008 The Kabbalah Centre International, Inc.

Kabbalah Publishing is a registered DBA of The Kabbalah Centre International, Inc.

For further information:

The Kabbalah Centre
155 E. 48th St., New York, NY 10017
1062 S. Robertson Blvd., Los Angeles, CA 90035

1.800.Kabbalah
www.kabbalah.com

First Edition
August 2008
Printed in USA
ISBN10: 1-57189-603-1
ISBN13: 978-1-57189-603-2

Design: HL Design (Hyun Min Lee) www.hldesignco.com

the way
of the
kabbalist

A User's Guide to Technology for the Soul™

www.kabbalah.com

Yehuda Berg

acknowledgement

To the people who make my life better each and every day: my parents, the Rav and Karen; my brother Michael; my wife Michal and our children.

table of contents

PART THREE: WORK WEEK

PART FOUR: MONTHLY CYCLE

PART FIVE: THE YEARLY CYCLE

PART SIX: GENERAL WAYS OF THE KABBALIST

introduction

Kabbalah is not a religion. Kabbalah is not a philosophy or a teaching. Kabbalah is a way of life: a living, breathing, vibrant pathway to the perfection of human beings and the transformation of the world. By perfection, I mean complete happiness free of worry, fear, anxiety, anger, and all other negative emotions that stand between us and fulfillment. Kabbalah is not restricted to any specific belief system or faith. It is universal. The same way the universal law of gravity keeps Muslims, Jews, Christians, and atheists grounded on the earth, Kabbalah's universal pathway elevates Muslims, Buddhists, Christians and all people to higher levels of fulfillment, wisdom, and authentic happiness.

The exciting news is that Kabbalah is not an all-or-nothing proposition. This book seeks to present a comprehensive pathway featuring as many elements of Kabbalah as possible. And that way, *you* decide which of Kabbalah's many tools and technologies you can best apply to your personal life.

The Cycles of Life

The structure of this book is based directly upon the recurring cycles of events that affect our lives. Accordingly, we will examine the role of Kabbalah in the day-to-day life of an individual, as well as the relevance of Kabbalah to our weekly, monthly and yearly activities. With every page you turn, remember, there is only one purpose behind Kabbalah's existence: to remove darkness from people's lives and transform the world into a place of unending fulfillment, serenity, and contentment. That's it. Kabbalah is not about becoming smarter or wiser. What good will it do you to become smarter if you're still miserable in your life? Nor is Kabbalah about becoming religious. More blood has been shed in the name of religion than for all other reasons combined. What good is being religious if one's prayers go unanswered?

Kabbalah is simply about increasing the level of Light in the world by tearing down the veils that create darkness. So let's explore what we mean by the terms *darkness* and *Light*.

Light and Dark

Life appears complicated, but it's not. *We* complicate our own lives. We create chaos out of order. We muck things up, continually making matters worse because we just don't understand what life is about or how it works.

The first thing we need to understand is that life is as simple as *darkness* and *Light*. I am not speaking metaphorically when I say *Light*. Nor am I using the word *darkness* allegorically. Only two things exist in this world: darkness and Light. Life appears complicated because darkness has a nearly endless variety of shades, and Light comes in countless colors. Nonetheless, at the heart of all that exists, you will either find darkness or Light.

From the time we are born, darkness and Light are all that exist. Our growth and increasing power are manifestations of Light. As we start to age, our gradually increasing weakness is an expression of darkness. Similarly, when we are content, full of passion, brimming with optimism and filled with the ultimate *I can achieve anything* attitude, this is Light expressing itself in our consciousness. These positive emotions are only the effect of Light, which itself is the underlying cause of all our happiness.

Conversely, when we are pessimistic, depressed, listless and cynical, these are manifestations of increased darkness in our consciousness. Again, these negative emotions are the Effect; darkness is the Cause.

Now if something external is causing our pain, such as a divorce or a sudden financial downturn, *this*, *too*, is an expression of increased darkness in our lives—but this time the darkness is affecting the world around us. Divorce is the Effect; the darkness that somehow crept into our lives is the Cause. In a similar way, when the right business deal comes along, when we happen to meet the girl of our dreams or Mr. Right, this means Light has come into our lives.

Our emotions, our state of mind, our state of consciousness, and every single event that unfolds around us is merely an expression of either the darkness or Light that we have invited into our lives.

There is nothing else.

For instance, when trying to find the right romantic partner, you have two options:

1. trial and error
2. increase the level of Light in your life.

From the Kabbalistic point of view, the second choice makes more sense. Why? Because if you have more Light, then the right partner will *automatically* enter your life. Light is the Cause; your soul mate is the Effect. Why go through the painful process of trial and error in order to find the right person?

The problem with humankind is that we have not been taught to think or live according to this simple paradigm. We live life by trial and error, never knowing that in truth it is all just as simple as darkness and Light.

These considerations lead us to a question that might be popping up in your mind right about now: How can we increase the quantity of Light in our lives? And, more importantly, where is this Light?

A World of Light

Our five senses frame—and therefore limit our perception of reality. Kabbalah says we perceive a mere 1 percent of reality because of our limited five senses. Yet the 99 percent that we do not perceive is precisely where all the Light exists! Within Kabbalah, this 99 Percent Reality is known by the Aramaic term *Zeir Anpin*. For the purposes of this book, we'll refer to it as both the World of Light and the 99 Percent Reality.

Relative to the 99 Percent Reality, our physical world is known by the Aramaic term *Malchut*, and we will refer to our world as the World of Darkness and the 1 Percent Reality. Just as the moon has no light of its own, our physical reality is devoid of spiritual Light. Just as the moon receives all of its light from the sun, all the happiness, wisdom, sustenance and fulfillment that occur in our world emanates from the 99 Percent Reality. Every song, story, invention and moment of happiness—even love itself—originates in the 99 Percent. Our world is simply the recipient, a Vessel that contains the Light of the 99 Percent.

Good things only happen in this world when we somehow manage to connect to the unseen World of Light. If this connection were not made, our world would be as dark, cold, and empty as deep space. When anything goes wrong in life it means we've disconnected from the World of Light. Disconnection happens all the time because most people have no idea that there is a World of Light that is the source of all happiness.

The Way of the Kabbalist is designed to help us make contact with the World of Light and to maintain that contact on a constant basis. We do this so we can use the Light to vanquish all darkness in our midst.

Each time these two worlds meet—when the 99 Percent and the 1 Percent combine to create 100 Percent—that is when spiritual Light goes on in the world. That is when everything goes right in life. That is when we feel passion, enthusiasm, and deep contentment. The only reason chaos exists anywhere in the world, the only reason darkness enters our personal lives, is because a curtain has been drawn across the Light, blocking it out. This curtain is the mechanism by which we disconnect from the source of pure joy. Yes, it's that simple.

Every technique and piece of technology that you encounter in this book offers a way to connect with the hidden World of Light by allowing you to tear down the curtain. When that curtain has been removed, the two realities become one. That is when you wake up to the world every day with untold delight and uncontainable excitement.

The Darkness of Death

As I mentioned earlier, Light comes in many colors, and darkness in many shades. If you were to make a list of all the things you dislike, that list would represent only a few of the countless shades of darkness. All the tools in this book are designed to banish every single shade of darkness. (By the way, the dimmest shade is death itself. In fact, that's what death is: pure, pitch-black darkness devoid of even a single sliver of Light.)

Would you believe that Kabbalah dared to make humankind the ultimate promise? Well, it's true. Kabbalah tells us that when we remove all shades of darkness from this physical world, death goes away with them. Immortality—the banishment of death—will become our new reality! This is the fondest desire of every person on earth, for it means freedom from that aspect of death that kills not only the body, but other parts of your life as well. When happiness gives way to sadness, it means death has slaughtered our happiness. When money stops flowing into our lives, the ancient Kabbalists tell us this means it has been dammed up by the force of death. When everything in life becomes confused and chaotic, the energy of death has momentarily trumped the perfect invisible force known as *order*. Allow me to quote my father, Kabbalist Rav Berg, who offered a simple explanation of immortality in his groundbreaking book *Nano: Technology of Mind Over Matter*:

When one speaks of immortality, it not only includes the end of biological death but it also incorporates unending joy, wisdom, happiness, excitement, passion, and fulfillment beyond what our rational minds can possibly conceive.

Immortality refers to a rapturous level of happiness that never leaves, never dies off.

Boredom, loneliness, sickness, anxiety, fear, worry, no longer exist for they are only the byproducts of death. From the Kabbalistic viewpoint, when you get to the essence of what all human beings want from life, it is immortality in all of its infinite manifestations.

At this point, another shade of darkness usually creeps into our consciousness: doubt, often joined by skepticism and cynicism. In other words, our inability to know with absolute certainty that death can be abolished is part of the darkness we face. *Doubt is darkness.* Because we all possess it in some measure, we cannot conceive that darkness—and therefore death—can be completely abolished forever. We seem to have found ourselves in a bit of a paradox! But we need not despair, because the wisdom of Kabbalah is designed to resolve this dilemma.

Here's how it works: The more you walk the "Way of the Kabbalist," the more Light you receive. The more Light you receive, the more certain you are that death can be eradicated from this world. Think of a child learning to walk. If she never believed she could do it, then she'd never get up on her feet. But with encouragement from her parents, she decides to take the risk. Then the very act of taking those first steps further supports her sense that she can do it. Soon she's walking; then she's speeding up and beginning to trot; and then she's running at full speed!

So it is with Kabbalah. The path itself gradually raises our consciousness so that we inevitably begin to perceive true reality, allowing us to embrace all the endless fulfillment this world really offers us.

The Power of Earning

According to Kabbalah, the Creator brought this dark and dangerous world into existence so that *we*—not God—could transform it into a Light-filled paradise where all humankind literally lives forever. This situation is not unlike that of the father who builds a billion-dollar business empire. His greatest joy would be to give his entire business to his son; however, if the father did so his son wouldn't really feel like the true owner. He couldn't feel fulfilled deep inside because everything had simply been handed to him. The son didn't start the business, or make it successful. He didn't prove himself worthy of assuming ownership of the entire empire. Thus, the only thing that *would* make the son truly happy would be if he could experience the joy, fulfillment, and sense of accomplishment that comes with building the empire himself.

Kabbalists call this idea *Bread of Shame*. This phrase acknowledges that everyone prefers to *earn* the bread they eat instead of receiving a charitable handout. A person who feels like a charity case feels a deep sense of shame. People feel truly worthy when they earn their rewards by virtue of their own efforts. This is a simple idea, but one with profound implications.

You see, immortality and paradise were handed over to us the moment we—the souls of humanity—were originally conceived, long before the existence of the physical universe. This *Endless World* consisted of two elements: the Light, which shines from the Creator, and the Vessel, an entity whose sole nature was to receive the Light of Happiness that flowed from the Creator.

But we chose not to receive the unending happiness that the Creator freely gave us. On the contrary, we asked for something far more valuable: The opportunity to build this paradise on our own instead of having it given to us, unearned, on a silver platter. This explains why God is concealed from our reality. God stepped aside and gave us the tools to build a paradise on our own. According to the ancient kabbalists, the moment when God stepped aside was the moment of the Big Bang creation of the universe.

Because we wanted to earn everything that the Light was giving to us freely, the original relationship between the Light and Vessel was suddenly broken. The Vessel was shattered, splitting into smaller pieces of souls (producing male and female souls) so that we could interact with one another for the purpose of re-creating paradise through our own efforts.

In simple terms, when we walk the pathway of Kabbalah, as outlined in this book, we slowly transform ourselves. This process of transformation has the larger effect of turning this world into paradise. But when we walk a path in the opposite direction, our world grows darker and the forces of chaos gather strength.

It doesn't take a genius to figure out that we've been walking the wrong path for the past few thousand years. The *way of the kabbalist* is the way *back home*. It is the way to earn and accomplish the ultimate goal, nothing less than never-ending happiness.

At first glance it might not be apparent that people who are following the way of the kabbalist are turning this world into a paradise. We cannot easily perceive this transformation with our five senses—and it is this very difficulty that gives the way of the kabbalist its extraordinary value making those who follow it worthy of inheriting immortality and Heaven on Earth. If we could see it all beforehand—if God abolished all our doubts by revealing the entire truth to us—then everyone could easily and readily walk the path, and the world would long ago have been transformed into paradise. But that would be no different from daddy handing you the keys to the executive boardroom without your having worked a single day in your life.

We can't create our own paradise if we don't have the free will to do so—or *not* to do so. And if we knew the truth it would be as if free will were abolished, because our choice would then be determined. So we are presented with curtains, and free will is preserved. Overcoming darkness, rising above doubt, surmounting cynicism and dumping disbelief—this is how we *earn* our inheritance so that we can enjoy it forever once we achieve it.

The Archenemy

As we struggle to earn our inheritance, we need to remember that our ignorance, our limited human perception, is not the only obstacle. We also have an enemy—only one, but a foe truly worthy of the role he plays. You know this adversary. You know this nemesis of humankind.

Satan.

Contrary to popular belief, Satan is not a devil or a demon with horns and a tail. Satan is a Hebrew word that makes its first appearance in the Bible, in the Old Testament, the original Torah scrolls of Moses. The word *Satan* simply means *Adversary.* Properly speaking, it's not a name; it's more of a job description. Satan is an adversarial force of consciousness that exists inside our heads. That's right; Satan is not some demon out in the world. He is a force of consciousness dwelling within our own minds.

Satan's job description is quite simple. He seeks one thing, and one thing only: He wants us to *receive unceasingly,* whereas our job is to *resist* receiving and start *sharing*—unconditionally. Why does Satan want us to receive? Because when we receive, we are reenacting our role in the Endless World. When all we do is receive, we might feel no lack in the moment. But later on—it could take an hour, a day, a month, or even a year—we feel *Bread of Shame* deep inside. More precisely, we disconnect from the 99 Percent Reality. That's what only receiving accomplishes. Our *Desire to Receive for the Self Alone*, as the kabbalists describe it, causes us to disconnect. Sharing, on the other hand, connects us to the Light of the 99 Percent.

So why do so many seem to love receiving and hate sharing? Enter the Adversary—our one and only archenemy. The Adversary expresses his will through the human ego. In fact, that's what the ego is: the voice of the Adversary taking control of our thoughts and desires. He is the curtain that conceals our true self—the human soul and our *Desire to Share* and to love others unconditionally.

The kabbalists revealed a frightening truth: Every thought, every impulse, every reactive emotion that ignites in our minds caused by the ego, is the tool of the Adversary. Those thoughts and emotions do not belong to us. We only think they do. In fact, the only time we make contact with our soul and true happiness is when we resist those thoughts. When we recognize the voice of the ego as the voice of the Adversary, we can then do something profound: the opposite of what the ego tells us to do. When we oppose the ego's bidding, we are no longer receiving. We are sharing.

Let's now see in more practical terms what it means to *receive*, what it means to *share*, and what it means to do the *opposite* of what the Adversary is compelling us to do.

Instead of yelling, we speak quietly.

Instead of cursing, we compliment.

Instead of taking, we give.

Instead of worrying, we awaken certainty and take charge.

Instead of fearing, we conjure up courage.

Instead of seeking revenge, we offer forgiveness.

Instead of blaming, we become accountable.

Instead of playing the victim, we hold ourselves responsible.

Instead of merely coping with a problem, we seek to cure it.

Instead of complaining, we start appreciating.

Instead of looking for the negative in a situation, we find the positive.

Instead of judging others, we look for the good in them.

Instead of gossiping and bad-mouthing others, we change the subject, or we simply walk away.

Instead of listing reasons why life is so unfair, we start counting our blessings.

Instead of calculating how something will benefit us, we figure out a way to ensure that the other party benefits.

Instead of reacting to external situations, we resist and become proactive.

Are you getting the picture? Good. My father has constantly stressed one point over the years, something we must never forget: all of this *opposite* behavior is not motivated by morals, ethics, or some noble ideal. Rather, we do it because it's smart business. It's shrewd behavior. It pays off. My father, the Rav, calls it *Enlightened Greed*. Make no mistake, it is greed, plain and simple—but not for fool's gold. It's greed for the real thing, for the Light itself. And this Enlightened Greed is the only reason for walking the kabbalistic path.

Time to See the Truth

If greed (albeit Enlightened Greed) is the motivation behind walking the kabbalistic path, you'd think more people would be kabbalists. After all, what could be easier or more intuitive than greed? The problem is, Satan throws us off track with one of his most powerful tricks: the illusion of time. When time passes between cause and effect, we can no longer see the connection; we lose sight of the true consequences of our actions.

Time is a curtain that conceals the amazing, mind-blowing rewards that sharing, caring behavior generates. Time also postpones the penalty produced by reactive, only-receiving behavior, leaving us with the false impression that selfishness pays off. Time, by delaying the consequences of our actions so that we are unable to connect the dots, creates the illusion that there is no justice.

Humankind has been deceived into selfish behavior for thousands of years by the concept of *time*. If we truly saw that hurting others only hurts ourselves down the road, we'd change, and fast. But we can't see the truth. Sure, we say that what goes around comes around, but in the depths of our being, most of us don't believe it. Furthermore, even when we know something is detrimental to our well-being, such as overeating, we don't have the willpower to overcome the relentless *Desire to Receive*. We eat and eat, even though we know we shouldn't.

The Adversary wields three kinds of power against us. First, the Adversary's goal is to prevent us from thinking long-term and to get us to settle for immediate gratification. He does this by using time to delay the repercussions of our actions. Then, when chaos and darkness strike in the future, they look like random events rather than being the result of our lost connection to the World of Light. However, there is in fact a profound order behind the appearance of randomness. Time merely conceals the true Cause-and-Effect relationship.

Secondly, the Adversary prevents us from believing that he actually exists, making it easier for us to succumb to the illusion that his impulses and desires belong to us. This is how he tricks us into following his marching orders all day long.

Thirdly, the Adversary is strong. Persuasive. Powerful. So defeating him is nearly impossible.

Yes, my friends, free will comes with a price. But *The Way of the Kabbalist* provides us with all the tools we need to address and surmount these three formidable obstacles.

We can't take this discussion any further at the moment because our archenemy's concealed workings and end goal will only become apparent to us as we begin to increase the amount of Light in our lives. However, reading this book and applying its contents to our lives is how we amplify the presence of Light, so let's get right to it. Darkness has reigned in this world long enough.

Let's begin in the womb.

part one
the cycles
of life

Pregnancy

Before a woman becomes pregnant, something must happen first: intercourse. Kabbalah tells us that intercourse between a man and a woman mirrors the potential intercourse that can take place between our World of Darkness and the World of Light. When these two worlds are connected, Light enters our reality.

The big secret, concealed for some two thousand years, is that individual people are intimately connected to the whole. The inner world within us and the outer world around us are constantly dancing with each other. What happens on the inside also happens on the outside. How? Because the original Vessel that received the Light—the Vessel that shattered into pieces, creating human souls—was structured along the lines of a hologram. The human body works the same way. A human being is made up of trillions upon trillions of cells, but every cell in your body contains the entire DNA code necessary to express your fully formed organism. The whole contains the part, and the part contains the whole; that's exactly how the shattered Vessel works. Each part contains the entire whole within it. Therefore, the most profound influence two people have upon the world is when they come together in a sexual relationship. Two people engaged in intercourse also contain the whole reality within them and this merger of souls is a merger of the Worlds of Darkness and the World of Light. Thus, their behavior also affects the whole.

The consciousness of each individual determines whether our world moves closer to the World of Light or whether it drifts deeper into darkness. If the consciousness of both parties is controlled by the Adversary and both are in a *receiving* or *selfish mode*, then the result will be greater distance between the 1 Percent and the 99 Percent. If both parties resist the impulses of the ego and raise their consciousnesses to the level of unconditional sharing, where each puts the other's needs ahead of one's own, our world will mirror this unselfish behavior and they will connect to the World of Light. Light will also flow into the couple's relationship, because they will be rewarded for contributing positive energy to our world.

All of our actions—both inside and outside the bedroom—determine whether or not our world connects to the World of Light. The human condition and the state of the planet are direct reflections of the deeds of every person on earth. As soon as we start to realize this truth and live by it, the world will change in miraculous ways.

The Moment of Conception

Another way to bring down Light into our reality is through children. Each time a man and woman join together in sexual relations, souls are brought down into this physical reality. If the couple achieves conception, then the soul enters into the woman the moment sperm fertilizes the egg.

The quality of soul, the brightness and degree of pure, positive consciousness that will eventually become expressed through a newborn baby, is determined by the consciousness and intent of the couple engaged in sexual relations. If the couple meditate with the intention of bringing down a soul that can help change the world and bring Light to this physical existence, the couple's thoughts rise up into the World of Light and attract the highest soul possible. Children often come into this world with a lot of baggage from past lives. Attracting a *high* soul means that the karma of a child (the result of its actions from past lives) is more balanced toward the positive side. This will ensure that the child's life is filled with less chaos and fewer difficult challenges. Some souls enter this world solely for the purpose of helping the world. Others come into the physical world to learn difficult lessons in life. Attracting a high soul ensures that he or she will be here to help rather than to learn.

A basic principle of Kabbalah is that *like attracts like*. If the couple engaging in sexual relations is filled with love, caring, and the desire to share unconditionally, they will attract a similar soul. Like attracts like. But if a couple's state of mind is governed by selfishness, anger, or lust, then the soul that is attracted to this union will have lots of spiritual work to do that could potentially be quite painful. When we understand the spiritual Laws of the Universe, we can use the spiritual technology of intercourse to help draw more positivity into our lives.

Spiritual DNA

According to Kabbalah, at the time of conception, at least 80 percent of the baby's future is determined. Another 10 percent of the baby's future is determined at the time of delivery. The remaining 10 percent is determined by the age of three. These three stages imprint a soul with its metaphysical DNA. This is why a couple's state of consciousness during intercourse is so important. Unfortunately, the Adversary did quite a good job of concealing these spiritual truths from the world. He has made the whole idea of spirituality foreign to our relentlessly rational minds. As a result, instead of focusing on what matters most—spirituality and consciousness—we believe that the information in our 1 Percent world offers us the only way to influence reality and protect our children.

The Power of Inner Light and Surrounding Light

At the moment of conception, the spiritual energy of the father instills within the aura of the embryo all of the potential the child can achieve in terms of spiritual transformation throughout his or her own life. Referred to as *Surrounding Light*, this illuminated encircling force remains in its state of potential, constantly pushing us to grow, develop, change, and transform. When we do, a portion of that Surrounding Light is transformed and actualized within us. The moment it is actualized, it becomes known as *Inner Light*.

At the time of conception the spiritual energy of the mother infuses the soul of the child with Inner Light, providing all the gifts, natural abilities and blessings that child will bring into this world and express throughout his or her own life.

Kabbalistic Meditations for Sexual Intercourse

The ancient *Zohar*—Kabbalah's most important text—provided us with unique meditations that we can use before or during intercourse to help us attract the most positive soul possible when we're trying to conceive children. If conception is not part of the couple's objective, they can still use these meditations to draw down positive souls for other people who are trying to have children all over the world. This will, in turn, generate increased Light (happiness, passion, and contentment) in their own lives and in the world at large. These techniques can help to ensure that positive souls will enter the lives of people throughout the world who are conceiving children but have no idea of the importance and power of how intention, meditation, and consciousness can influence their sexual union and conception.

The original meditations in the *Zohar* were written in the ancient language of Aramaic. Aramaic is a powerful divine alphabet that reaches the World of Light, avoiding any obstructions or blockages that dwell between the two worlds. The *Zohar* explains that there are both positive and negative packets of energy in the spiritual atmosphere. These packets of energy are actual forces of consciousness, also known as *angels*. Angels understand almost all the languages of humankind. Thus, negative angels often interrupt the prayers uttered by humankind, preventing the words from ascending into the 99 Percent Reality. Aramaic is the one language that angels do not understand, so any prayer or meditation uttered in Aramaic ascends unhindered into the highest realm of the spiritual worlds.

For this reason, the great kabbalists of history used Aramaic for all the most important prayer-connections. This is why the great Kabbalist Rav Shimon bar Yochai wrote the *Zohar*, the most important book of Kabbalah, in Aramaic. Jesus and the great kabbalists of history spoke and wrote in Aramaic.

Aramaic has an innate ability to penetrate directly into the World of Light.

Meditations Prior to Intercourse

Below is a transliteration of the ancient Aramaic meditation used prior to intercourse, together with its original Aramaic form. You can scan the Aramaic form visually from right to left, line by line, or you can read the transliteration. This meditation ensures that our thoughts remain pure and positive during intercourse. It blocks out unwanted negative thoughts so that sharing and unconditional love fills our minds during this important interaction.

A TRANSLITERATION OF KABBALISTIC BLESSING

עֲטִיפָא בְּקִטְפָא אִזְדַּמְנַת, שָׁאֲרֵי שָׁאֲרֵי, לָא תִּעוֹל וְלָא תִּנְפּוֹק,
לָא דִּידָךְ וְלָא בְּעַדְבָּךְ. תּוּב תּוּב, יַמָּא אִתְרְגִישָׁא, גַּלְגַּלּוֹי לִיךְ קָרָאן,
בְּחוּלָקָא קַדִּישָׁא אֲחִידְנָא, בִּקְדוּשָׁה דְּמַלְכָּא אִתְעַטַּפְנָא.

Atifa bekitfa izdamnat, sharei sharei, la ti'ol vela tinpok, la didach
vela be'advach. tuv tuv, yama itregisha, galgaloy lich karan,
bechulaka kadisha achidna, bikdusha demalka itatafna.

Uniting the Two Worlds

The meditation below unites the Upper World of Light, where 99 Percent of reality exists, with our Lower World of Darkness, the physical 1 Percent world we perceive with our five senses. This unification between these two realities takes place when the female soul unites with the male soul during intercourse. Light fills the couple, and Light fills our entire world. You can meditate upon this two-letter sequence prior to intercourse; or, if you have a good memory, memorize the letters and then visualize them at the moment of orgasm.

The first letter is called VAV.
This letter connects to the World of Light, *Zeir Anpin*.

The second letter is called HEI.
This letter connects to the World of Darkness, our physical reality, *Malchut*.

When you visualize *both* letters in your mind's eye, the spiritual World of Light merges with our physical World of Darkness. The two realities become *one reality*, just as the two members of a couple become *one soul* during sexual relations. And like the light of a lamp eradicating darkness from a room, when the two worlds merge the Light from the unseen spiritual reality banishes all darkness in our world.

Kabbalah teaches that children choose their parents. Many criteria go into this choice, including karma, the DNA of the parents, and the social, physical, and emotional characteristics of the parents. Given that like attracts like, a child soul will select parents who will give them the best opportunity to complete their own transformation in their lifetime. On the other side of the equation, the parents' intentions during intercourse will create an affinity with the spiritual needs of the child. If both parents are striving for greater spiritual growth, they will attract a soul who also seeks spiritual transformation.

The Nine Months of Pregnancy

When you add up the numerical values of the letters in the Hebrew word for pregnancy (*herayon*), you find that the word has an overall numerical value of 271. This number is significant because it corresponds to the 271 days (or nine months) required for a soul to completely infuse an embryo and produce a newborn baby.

There is a reason why it takes nine months for a baby to grow from conception to birth. First, you must know that reality is composed of ten dimensions known as the Ten *Sefirot* or Ten Emanations. Their names are:

1. *Keter*
2. *Chochmah*
3. *Binah*
4. *Chesed*
5. *Gevurah*   **Nine dimensions
nine months**
6. *Tiferet*
7. *Netzach*
8. *Hod*
9. *Yesod*—Cosmic Womb
10. *Malchut*—Physical Reality

As mentioned previously, the tenth dimension, *Malchut*, represents our physical reality. During the nine months of gestation, the soul travels through the nine dimensions of the spiritual world, from *Keter* to *Yesod*, which is the cosmic womb. Once this process is complete, the soul enters physical reality, and simultaneously, the infant emerges from the womb.

The Three-Column System

There is another way of explaining the spiritual system that governs our world. According to Kabbalah, reality is founded upon three forces of energy, known as the Three-Column System. The Right Column is the positive (+) charge, an outward-directed, sharing force of energy; the Left Column is the negative (-) charge, a receiving energy; and the Central Column is the neutral component mediating between the two, determining how much *imparting* (+) and how much *receiving* (-) is taking place. For a circuitry of energy to be whole and complete, all three components are required.

The language of two thousand years ago sometimes sounds as though it has no place in our modern world, but today science confirms this ancient kabbalistic view of reality. Particle physicists tell us that the world is built on three distinct particles: the proton (+), the electron (-), and the neutron. Together, these three subatomic particles form the atom, our basic building block of the material world.

In simple terms, the World of Light corresponds to the Right Column, and the World of Darkness is the Left Column. Our free will (human consciousness) determines whether the two worlds will unite to create a perfect illuminating structure of energy. Since each of the Three Columns of *energy* also contains a Right, Left and Central Column, all three columns and their sub-columns must be included in order for an entity to be complete. This is why a pregnancy lasts nine months: the number nine corresponds to the three sub-columns inside the three major columns, 3 x 3 = 9.

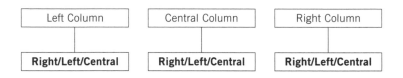

So the nine months of pregnancy, which correspond to the nine columns and sub-columns that form the universe, ensure that an embryo develops all the physical and spiritual components necessary to produce a viable newborn baby.

During these nine months, as the baby develops the soul learns all the secrets of the universe. The baby's entire life to come is shown to it, along with its past lives, too. Just prior to its birth, an angel taps the child above the upper lip, causing the child to forget everything. This is the reason for the vertical groove we all have between our noses and our upper lips.

On a subconscious level, the child knows what it came into this world to achieve. However, the rational mind and the ego will do everything in their power to prevent the soul from remembering its purpose and acting to fulfill it. Like other obstacles we've discussed, the opposition of the ego and rational mind exist for the purpose of permitting free will.

As noted at the outset of this book, we came here to earn and accomplish the transformation of our world into a full-fledged paradise by our own effort. The ego and rational mind, which fill us with selfishness, doubt, and cynicism are the forces we struggle against in our effort to make contact with our soul and the memory that lingers deep within us. As we connect to our soul and achieve our life purpose, we unite the World of Darkness with the World of Light, increasing the amount of positive energy in our lives.

The First Three Months of Pregnancy

During the first three months of pregnancy, the developing embryo is at its most vulnerable, because all three columns have not yet been developed. For this reason, kabbalists advise us to not reveal the pregnancy to anyone during this time. Envious stares, jealous glances, or any kind of ill will, intentional or unintentional, can harm the fetus. After three months have passed, it is safe to share the good news with family and friends. Kabbalah also suggests that mothers work hard to keep their consciousness in a positive, elevated state during this critical period when every emotion, action, and even the words one speaks can directly influence the developing fetus and emerging soul.

Unfortunately, pregnancy is a time when a woman's hormones wreak havoc upon her nerves. The body aches, the stomach is queasy, and the mother is often tired and moody. The kabbalistic work during pregnancy is to *resist* the temptation to succumb to these states of mind and to instead rise above them. The more one resists inner negativity, the more Light the soul receives.

The Healing, Cleansing Power of Water

During pregnancy a woman is advised to use an ancient tool known as the *mikveh*. The *mikveh* is a special kind of bath, which helps purify, cleanse, and empower both the mother and the developing embryo. It removes all negative metaphysical forces that try to attach to the child and the mother. *Mikvehs*, found in many cities throughout the world, are constructed according to precise measurements and principles outlined by the ancient kabbalists. Why do *mikvehs* use water? Water is the closest earthly form that resembles the spiritual essence of the Light of the Creator, which is why our bodies are more than 70 percent water. Think of water as a form of *liquid Light*. Therefore, if the body is completely immersed so that not even a single hair remains outside of the water, all forms of darkness, both physical and spiritual, are washed away.

The *Zohar* teaches that negative forces literally penetrate to the level of our cells. In addition, the consciousness of a negative force is *receiving*, so the negative force sucks the life force of Light out of each cell. Once a single cell is depleted of energy the negative force moves onto a second cell, and so on. Immersion in the *mikveh* eradicates these negative entities from our very being.

Just as a newborn infant emerges from the womb of its mother into a new life, when we emerge from the *mivkeh*—which is like a cosmic womb—we are born anew. The only way negativity and darkness can once again attach themselves to us is if we begin reacting and succumbing to the urgings of the Adversary, the ego. Otherwise, after using the technology of the *mikveh* we are healthy, brand-new human beings. Many people who use the *mikveh* do not know that this technology has such a powerful effect. Once they leave the *mikveh*, they revert to their old ways and thoughts, and negativity is given an opening to jump back in.

Labor

During labor, the mother and father can meditate upon the following kabbalistic verse, and the 72 Names of God to help ease the pain of childbirth and support a smoother delivery:

לַמְנַצֵּחַ מִזְמוֹר לְדָוִד:
leDavid mizmor Lamnatze'ach

יַעַנְךָ יְהוָה בְּיוֹם צָרָה יְשַׂגֶּבְךָ שֵׁם אֱלֹהֵי יַעֲקֹב:
Ya'acov Elohei shem yesagevcha tzara beyom Adonai Ya'anecha

יִשְׁלַח־עֶזְרְךָ מִקֹּדֶשׁ וּמִצִּיּוֹן יִסְעָדֶךָּ:
yisadeka umi'Tziyon mikodesh ezrecha Yishlach

יִזְכֹּר כָּל־מִנְחֹתֶךָ וְעוֹלָתְךָ יְדַשְּׁנֶה סֶלָה:
sela yedashneh ve'olatcha minchotecha kol Yizkor

יִתֶּן־לְךָ כִלְבָבֶךָ וְכָל־עֲצָתְךָ יְמַלֵּא:
yemale atzat'cha vechol chilvavecha lecha Yiten

נְרַנְּנָה בִּישׁוּעָתֶךָ וּבְשֵׁם־אֱלֹהֵינוּ נִדְגֹּל יְמַלֵּא יְהוָה כָּל־מִשְׁאֲלוֹתֶיךָ:
mish'alotecha kol Adonai yemale nidgol Eloheinu uvshem bishu'atecha Neranena

עַתָּה יָדַעְתִּי כִּי הוֹשִׁיעַ יְהוָה מְשִׁיחוֹ יַעֲנֵהוּ מִשְּׁמֵי קָדְשׁוֹ בִּגְבֻרוֹת יֵשַׁע יְמִינוֹ:
yemino yesha bigvurot kodsho mishmei ya'anehu meshicho Adonai hoshi'a ki yadati Ata

אֵלֶּה בָרֶכֶב וְאֵלֶּה בַסּוּסִים וַאֲנַחְנוּ בְּשֵׁם־יְהוָה אֱלֹהֵינוּ נַזְכִּיר:
nazkir Eloheinu Adonai beshem va'anachnu vasusim ve'eleh varechev Eleh

הֵמָּה כָּרְעוּ וְנָפָלוּ וַאֲנַחְנוּ קַמְנוּ וַנִּתְעוֹדָד:
vanit'odad kamnu va'anachnu hefafalu karu Hema

יְהוָה הוֹשִׁיעָה הַמֶּלֶךְ יַעֲנֵנוּ בְיוֹם־קָרְאֵנוּ:
korenu veyom ya'anenu hamelech hoshi'a Adonai

Spiritually speaking, the longer a pregnancy lasts and the more natural the labor process, the better it will be for the child. If any kind of operation is performed on a firstborn male child, the Redemption of the Firstborn (*Pidyon HaBen* explained in the next chapter) cannot be performed. Thus every attempt should be made to have children naturally, unless the safety of the mother and/or child are at risk.

If either the mother or the father reads the *Zohar* in addition to the above meditations, before and during labor, a protective shield of Light will be generated, helping to ensure a safe and Light-filled delivery.

Birth

Peace Be upon the Male
(*Shalom Zachar*)

After the first Friday night Sabbath meal since the birth of the newborn male child, the family participates in a spiritual connection
called *Shalom Zachar*. This powerful connection takes place on
the Sabbath *before* what is known as the Covenant of Circumcision
(explained in the next section). This allows the child to experience
one complete Sabbath before circumcision is performed. Sabbath
is the source of all the energy and power that the baby will receive
from the circumcision on a seed level. Just as an apple seed contains the entire apple tree, including the final fruit, the Sabbath
prior to the circumcision contains all of the energy, Light and
power that the child will receive during the circumcision.

In this connection, everyone eats a chickpea. If you look closely at
a chickpea, you will see two lips that look similar to a child's
mouth. The idea behind eating the chickpea is that you are
empowering the child to speak the true words of wisdom that he
already knows in the depth of his soul. Remember that while in the
womb the child is shown all the secrets of the universe, all of his
past life experiences, and—most importantly—the various
moments of transformation he needs to achieve during his upcoming life. However, to preserve the child's free will, an angel erases
the child's memory of everything he or she has just learned.

As people participating in the *Shalom Zachar* eat the chickpea,
they meditate upon the child, empowering him with strength,
intuition and courage to instinctively remember, recognize and
embrace all the challenges that he came to this world to conquer
in order to achieve personal transformation. The *Shalom
Zachar* helps the child subconsciously remember all that he

forgot as he emerged from the womb. The child will have the ability to recall and thus *speak* powerful truths. Participants eating the chickpea also receive an awareness of their own mission in life.

The Covenant of Circumcision

Circumcision is known in Hebrew as *Brit Milah*. Circumcision is not merely a custom or a religious ritual performed for the sake of tradition. Circumcision is a powerful technology that offers us the ability to banish the strongest negative forces that penetrate our physical reality and our personal lives.

As we stated before, the human body mirrors spiritual reality, which is composed of ten dimensions or *Sefirot*. The male reproductive organ corresponds to the *Sefirah* of *Yesod*, which is the portal and gateway that leads into our physical reality. All spiritual Light that enters our world travels through *Yesod*. For this reason, negative entities hover at the gateway of *Yesod* to snatch away Light and gain entrance into our lives.

- *Keter*
- *Chochmah*
- *Binah* ⟷ **Source of Life**
- *Chesed*
- *Gevurah*
- *Tiferet*
- *Netzach*
- *Hod*
- *Yesod* ⟷ **Gateway into our World**
- *Malchut* — Physical Reality

In the male body, the reproductive organ is the physical manifestation of *Yesod*. Semen resembles the Light of the Creator in its power to give life, and flows through the male anatomy into the female reproductive organ, mirroring the Light that flows through *Yesod* into *Malchut*, the physical world. Waste products also flow through the male reproductive organ, which is a reflection of the negative forces that hover in *Yesod*, waiting for a chance to penetrate our lives. Thus, the male organ contains both the highest level of divinity (semen, which entails the power to create a human life) and the darkest form of physicality (human waste).

The purpose of circumcision is to tear away the dark, negative entities that reside in the dimension of *Yesod*. Because the human body is a pure microcosm of the spiritual realm, circumcising the *Yesod*, in the form of the male reproductive organ, annihilates the negative forces (the foreskin) that dwell in this hidden dimension.

Modern medical science has found evidence validating the spiritual truth of the negativity of the foreskin. Scientists have proven that HIV binds easily to the cells of the foreskin. Using descriptive language profoundly similar to Kabbalah, scientists say that the foreskin acts as a portal for HIV to enter into the body and have also found that the inner foreskin is nine times more susceptible to the virus than the outer layers.

Circumcision is performed on the eighth day after the male child is born. This allows the soul of the child time to connect with the spiritual dimension known as *Binah*, which is eight levels higher than *Malchut*. *Binah*, also known as the *Tree of Life Reality*, is the storehouse of Light that is the source of life. Waiting for the eighth day also allows the child to experience one complete Sabbath before circumcision, which further connects the child to *Binah*.

It is interesting to note that medical science tells us that on the eighth day of life a baby's blood starts clotting. Kabbalah tells us that the soul resides in the blood and contains both positive and negative aspects. If the negative aspect of death remains in the blood of a child, as he grows up, the Adversary will have the power to influence the child's thoughts, decisions and choices in destructive ways. Through the circumcision, the blood is cleansed spiritually, and the negative force is literally cut out.

Prior to the circumcision a chair is set for the famed righteous sage, Elijah the Prophet. This great biblical prophet is the one who taught the divine teachings of the *Zohar* to Rav Shimon bar Yochai some two thousand years ago. The metaphysical presence of Elijah eradicates the negative energy and forces of death during the circumcision.

Elijah cannot dwell among people who have any level of negativity within them. However, each of us clearly has some measure of ego and negativity; therefore, during the circumcision, the Creator literally purifies all those in attendance so that Elijah can be present to banish the death force from the child. In this way each person attending a circumcision is automatically spiritually cleansed and purified.

Someone is chosen to hold the child during the circumcision. A spiritual teacher or kabbalist, known as a *Sondok*, is usually chosen for this function. Whereas Elijah the Prophet's role is to eliminate the forces of darkness and death, the *Sondok* channels the Light that will fortify and strengthen the child. The amount of energy and consciousness put into the circumcision determines how strong the child will be throughout his life, particularly with regard to his immune system and his level of consciousness.

At the conclusion of the circumcision, the foreskin, source of all negativity and death, is buried in the ground.

Perhaps the most important effect of the Covenant of Circumcision is that *everyone* attending this connection receives spiritual Light, blessings, purification and transformation equal to that achieved by forty days of fasting. In this way circumcision is the ultimate win-win-win scenario for the baby, the family, and all the participants. Kabbalists attend these events not to enjoy a party, but rather to remove death's negativity from themselves and others, and to strengthen their own connection to the Tree of Life.

The Redemption of the Firstborn

Firstborn male children offer us a powerful opportunity to perform what is known as *The Redemption of the Firstborn* (*Pidyon Haben* in Hebrew) thirty days after the birth. This ancient kabbalistic practice actually removes the Angel of Death from the firstborn child, as well as all future siblings who enter into the family, and from all those who participate in the event. Just as an orange seed directly influences the trunk, branches, leaves, and fruit that emerge from it, a firstborn child spiritually influences all the children that follow him. Thus, by removing "death aspect" from the firstborn, the force of death is removed from all the children that follow. God gave Moses the Redemption of the Firstborn *before* the revelation of the Torah on Mount Sinai. Jesus (*Yehoshua*) was redeemed according to this ancient practice by his parents Miriam and Yosef (Mary and Joseph), who took him to the Temple to perform this kabbalistic rite.

If a woman delivers a first child naturally—meaning that she has never had a miscarriage after the third month of pregnancy, and her first child is not delivered by cesarean section—and the child is a male, then the child's father performs the Redemption of the Firstborn. The ancient Kabbalist Rav Isaac Luria explains that when a firstborn male is born into this world naturally, the Angel of Death attaches himself to the child. The Redemption of the Firstborn, however, provides the technology for the Angel of Death to be removed from the child and transferred to the *Kohen*, who is a descendant of the High Priests. This is accomplished by the *Kohen* receiving "ownership" of the baby, where the life energy of the *Kohen* is imbued within the baby and separates him from the Angel of Death. This is followed by the father buying the baby back from the *Kohen* for the redemptive value of five silver coins, which removes the Angel of Death from the child and transfers that destructive energy to the *Kohen*. A *Kohen*'s inner spiritual structure allows him to withstand the temporary infusion of the death energy that is transferred to him from the child through the exchange of the coins.

Contrary to popular belief, the actions involved in this procedure are not symbolic. Nor are they mere traditions or acts of remembrance. Rather, we are speaking of an ancient technology for removing the influence of the Angel of Death from the life of the child and from all of the participants attending. The main reason to attend such an event (beyond supporting friends and family) is to remove the death force from oneself.

Knowing is the connection. By expecting and demanding nothing less than the removal of the death force, we activate the mechanism that allows us to receive this profound power. Participating in this ceremony is equivalent to eighty four consecutive days of fasting. If one merely performs the Redemption of the Firstborn for the sake of tradition, the Angel of Death remains untouched. He is free to exert his dark influence over the child and his siblings throughout their lives.

The Naming of the Girl

The naming of a male child occurs during the Covenant of Circumcision, but when the newborn child is female, there is a baby naming for the child on her second *Shabbat*. This allows her to experience one complete *Shabbat* without a name, so that her soul has time to infuse completely into her body before her name is given.

The secret purpose and power of a name is found in the Hebrew word for "soul," which is *Neshamah*. At the root or center of the word we find another Hebrew word, which is, *Shem*, or "name." A Kabbalist will never name a child after a dead relative because the emotional, spiritual, and physical baggage of that person would be automatically transferred to the child through the name, since the name of a person contains the metaphysical DNA of the soul. A child's name instills certain characteristics within him or her that will affect his or her spiritual and physical growth and development throughout his or her life. Thus, a *baby naming* is a profoundly important event.

According to the sages, names for a child are best chosen from among the great giants of Torah who were conduits for the revelation of Light in this world. This is not for purposes of tradition or honoring the dead. Rather, the particular letters of the alphabet that compose a specific name in the Torah possess precise qualities that will shape and influence a child to whom that name is given. Since the special character traits of great spiritual leaders are contained within their names, these names are given to children to help them achieve their own spiritual transformations. The naming of a male child occurs during the Covenant of Circumcision.

Childhood

The First Hair Cut

Kabbalistically, hair serves as an antenna that draws down the spiritual Light permeating all the hidden dimensions—also known as The Tree of Life Reality or the World of Light, the 99 Percent. Because of the ability of hair to attract and capture these spiritual forces, kabbalists do not cut a newborn male baby's hair for the first three years of his life. This time period corresponds to the Three Column System, so the entire three years is necessary to establish a complete structure of energy. During this time, the hair is drawing down enough spiritual power so that the child's body and soul are complete, and filled with divine energy.

The structure being developed within the child during this time is known as a Spiritual Vessel, or Desire. A Vessel is a person's ability to contain the Light that will bring him happiness throughout his life. *The greater a person's desire for the Light, the greater the amount of Light that is revealed.* For this reason, parents should resist saying no to a child during the first three years of life. Instead, if misbehaving, a child's attention should be redirected. The more the child feels free to desire anything during the first three years, the stronger the Vessel he will build. At age three the child's hair is cut, thereby completing the infusion of energy.

This first haircut imbues the child with the power of *resistance*. Resistance is the key to exercising free will and to attaining happiness; it's a behavioral tool we use throughout life to connect to the Light. When we resist the ego, and resist our tendency to simply react to circumstances without consideration, we connect to Light. Although *resistance* is a simple concept, it is very difficult to employ. Human nature is governed by reactivity, selfish desire, and the ego. Overcoming these is lifelong work.

The cutting of the hair is usually performed with friends and family present. This allows all the participants to share in the same energy and power that the child is receiving. Now, properly imbued with the power of resistance, the child will grow up with the ability to resist ego, selfishness, reactivity, and all negative desires so that he can more readily connect to the World of Light.

Parents and Children

Children choose their parents prior to conception. When a soul is in the Upper World, it chooses parents who will be able to provide it with the spiritual and physical DNA necessary for the child to achieve the personal transformation for which it comes into this life. Both the child and its parents create for each other the opportunity to grow, evolve, and transform. These opportunities are especially obvious during parent-child conflicts.

Conflicts occur for one reason: there is a lesson for *both* parties to learn. Each of us comes into this world with a specific set of reactive, self-centered character traits that lie deep within us, and manifest on the surface. Our relationships serve one purpose—to push our buttons and thereby reveal the qualities implanted within our nature that we came into this life to resolve. When children upset their parents, and parents upset their children, both are being presented with an opportunity to identify their own particular negative attributes and tendencies. When we ignore our negative traits, when we do not tend to the conflicts that inevitably erupt within the family, we disconnect from the World of Light and our personal lives grow darker. On the other hand, each time we identify a negative trait, and take responsibility for it, and put forth the necessary effort to transform it, we connect to the World of Light and our lives get better. Naturally it's tempting to blame our parents or blame our children for our chaos. However, blaming others moves us in the wrong direction. Becoming accountable for everything is the essence of true transformation.

This is why it is so important for parents to identify the spiritual corrections and transformations that their children must experience in life, and why it's important for parents to give their children the spiritual tools they will need to succeed. Providing these spiritual tools is the reason Kabbalah was revealed to mankind.

When our children succeed spiritually, they also succeed in the physical world, enjoying happiness, fulfillment, dignity and independence. If our children fail spiritually they might appear to be succeeding "materially," but they will still be unfulfilled. By depending on external factors for their own happiness, they will have relinquished control over their own lives.

As we parents come to see that we are accountable for all the conflicts we have with our children, it becomes clear that we must lay down the rules of the household, always speaking with one voice when it comes to discipline. In an effort to get their own way, children instinctively try to work the seams between their parents. "Divide and conquer" is a tactic children have used since the dawn of time. Parents should make every attempt to remain united (even if one of the parents is off the mark) when dealing with children. Differences can be sorted out between parents in private, at a later time. In the context of the child, consistency and love are far more important than right and wrong.

When children see unwavering unity and love between their parents, this will instill a higher consciousness and deep sense of fulfillment within them. The path to happiness is not based on winning arguments at home. It is based on purity of being and the amount of unconditional love we can share with another human being. When parents serve as role models for unconditional love and unity, when they truly walk the walk, their children will develop the same type of behavior.

Family

Each of us comes into this world with a specific set of spiritual goals that must be achieved over the course of our lifetimes. These changes take place within the individual, but are not limited to the individual. As mentioned previously, our children not only inherit our DNA, they also inherit a portion of our consciousness. In fact, DNA, molecules and atoms are all really different levels of consciousness. Thus, each time a parent changes, changes are also taking place in their children.

Likewise, when children embrace spirituality, beginning at the age of twelve and thirteen, any transformation they undergo will also influence their parents. A spiritual umbilical cord forever links parents, children and siblings. When one boat rises, everyone experiences a bit of that new elevation; when one falls, everyone in the family sinks a little bit. The purpose of a family is to create an opportunity for constant interactions that allow us to discover those places within us where self-centered desire governs our behavior. Family members have the annoying talent of triggering reactions within us, *thereby giving us an opportunity not to react.*

Each time we forgo a selfish desire and choose selfless behavior—each time we *choose* our response instead of reacting—we make a change in our lives. And with each change, we receive a little more Light. As we've seen, our efforts benefit our families as well, giving them additional strength to identify and transform their own selfishness. And as a family experiences the power of spiritual transformation and connects to the World of Light, those benefits extend to its friends, neighbors, and community. As people throughout the world succeed in moving away from the dictates of the ego and toward selflessness, the entire planet is transformed into a paradise. This is the purpose of life, and the tools offered by Kabbalah can help us achieve that goal.

Bar Mitzvah/Bat Mitzvah

Child	Active	*Nefesh*	Birth to age thirteen: pure Desire to Receive is awakened and developed. Body consciousness.
Adolescent	Reactive	*Ruach*	Age thirteen to twenty: awakening of an awareness of sharing, becoming reactive. The spirit of rebellion ignites, along with the desire to earn and achieve.
Adult	Proactive	*Neshama*	Age twenty and beyond: reaching the level of a "self-sustaining" individual and the capacity for parenthood and true sharing. Soul consciousness.

From the kabbalistic perspective, the journey of life is simple. We are born into this world *active*. All our actions and behaviors are designed to ignite the dormant desires of the body as we acclimate to the world around us. As we grow older, we become *reactive*. Our desires are now strong and we react to their every impulse and urge. We are now essentially automatic in our response to the reactive desires that burn within us. Eventually we realize that the way to achieve our spiritual goals in life is to transform from reactive adults into *proactive* people. Proactive, we become the cause of our own behavior and take control of our own consciousness. Instead of being directed by our desires, we master them. This way of being connects us to the 99 Percent Reality, whereas reactive behavior disconnects us from this realm. These three types of consciousness we are exploring—active, reactive, proactive—ignite within us at various levels of the human soul.

When a child comes into this world, the aspect of the soul known as *Nefesh*—Crude Spirit—is activated. This aspect is governed by the consciousness of pure receiving, and motivates the child from birth to age thirteen for boys, twelve for girls. This is the stage we described above, during which time the consciousness of the child is considered to be active.

Adolescence begins at age thirteen and the aspect of soul called *Ruach* fires up. Now we feel the urge to earn and achieve, but it is based on reactive impulses. We begin to understand the concept of sharing, but when it is painful or uncomfortable we do not yet have the power to truly share. The desire to rebel or revolt ignites within us, but this desire is primarily motivated by self-interest. Only in the next stage do we realize that the only rebellion worth engaging in is the one against our internal enemy—self interest.

From age twenty onward we begin to direct our consciousness toward self-transformation, for now we see that the only way to achieve the fulfillment that is our destiny is by virtue of our own effort. This consciousness is channeled through the aspect of the soul called *Neshamah*, the highest and purest level of soul.

Without question, the *Bar/Batmitzvah* is the least understood form of spiritual connection. Most people today consider the *Bar/Batmitzvah* a time for partying and celebrating the arrival of adulthood for a child. Kabbalistically, however, the Bar/Batmitzvah is understood as a tool for the awakening of *free will* and personal accountability. According to Kabbalah, up until the age of twelve for a girl and thirteen for a boy, children have no free will; they are still developing those aspects of themselves that are based in self-centered desire and a reactive nature. This provides us with an egocentric character that can be overcome and transformed during adult life. Once we have a fully-formed selfish nature, we can exercise our free will by resisting it, thereby earning a connection to the World of Light. In other words, instead of having paradise handed to us carte blanch like a charitable handout, our selfish nature gives us an opportunity to be worthy of the unending happiness that is our ultimate destiny.

Prior to the *Bar/Batmitzvah*, a child is not held accountable for his or her choices; that responsibility falls to the parents. After the *Bar/Batmitzvah*, the individual gains the power of free will and becomes responsible for every decision he or she makes.

A higher aspect of the human soul is awakened. (By the way, the terms *consciousness* and *soul* are near interchangeable in Kabbalah since a soul is made up of consciousness.) Thus, through the *Bar/Batmitzvah*, the child receives an additional infusion of soul or consciousness that provides the intellectual and spiritual capacity to recognize one's reactive impulses, as well as the power to resist them.

The child's state of consciousness or soul prior to the *Bar/Batmitzvah* is known in Hebrew as *Nefesh*. The state of consciousness or soul that is ignited at age twelve or thirteen is called *Ruach*. The first letters of these two words, *Nun* and *Reish*, together form the Hebrew word *ner*, which means "candle." Merely by its presence, a candle has the power to diminish the darkness in a room. When children undergo their *Bar/Batmitzvah*, they receive the ability to banish darkness from their lives. If they do not make use of this power, they will wind up injecting more darkness into their lives.

If teens do not understand the true nature of reality and how these spiritual tools work, they will reflexively feed selfish desire. This is the cause of the depression and mood swings that most teens suffer. They disconnect from the World of Light and turn to drugs, alcohol, sex, and other activities that give them a taste of Light but eventually cause them to disconnect.

Adulthood

Male and Female Energy

Male and female souls correspond to the original Light and Vessel that existed prior to the creation of the physical universe. When the Vessel was originally created by the Light of the Creator, the Vessel's sole nature was one of *receiving*. This force of receiving is similar to the negative pole (-) on a battery. The Vessel's function and nature was to receive the Light of Happiness emanating from the Creator. However, just as we inherit traits from our parents, the Vessel also inherited an aspect of the Light. The Vessel inherited a positive force (+), similar to the positive pole on a battery. Male energy is the DNA inherited by the Vessel, the positive pole. Female energy is the divine receiving nature of the Vessel created by the Light, the negative pole. Both are contained within the one Vessel.

When the Vessel shattered, its male aspect was separated from its female counterpart, creating individual male and female souls. These then shattered once more into countless sparks of souls. This accounts for the origin of all the male and female souls on earth—past, present and future. Consequently, from the kabbalistic point of view, a male soul is merely half of a soul, as is a female soul. A complete soul contains both male and female aspects, therefore, the purpose of life is to find our other half so that we can be complete. This is the underlying cause of the sexual attraction between men and women. Each soul is seeking to return to the World of Light by reuniting with its soul mate.

How does one find his or her true soul mate? When we are about to complete our transformation from reactive self-centered beings into proactive, selfless individuals, we earn the appearance of our soul mate; he or she shows up in our lives. There is no other way. Every relationship we have prior to this moment is merely a step on the path to our ultimate destination. No relationship, even if it ends up in divorce, is a mistake. Every relationship serves a profound purpose by taking us closer to our true soul mate, provided we take the opportunity to transform our nature by learning from our mistakes. If we don't learn from our mistakes, we'll wind up in another relationship that will merely be a repeat of those lessons that came before. Only the names and faces will be different.

Like a light bulb which shines only when a filament acts as a conduit between positive and negative poles, marriage is a technology, a metaphysical procedure for bonding two halves of one soul. As we've noted, the man corresponds to the positive pole, a woman corresponds to the negative pole, and the marriage contract (known in kabbalistic language as a *Ketubah*) is the filament that brings the two poles together. The *Ketubah* creates a circuit of energy so that spiritual Light shines in the marriage. If we walk the way of the kabbalist and look within instead of blaming others, we can build a *virtual* soul mate relationship with our current partner, thus achieving deep happiness and contentment.

Part of the kabbalistic marriage connection consists of what kabbalists call *The Conditions before Creation*. These *Conditions* are performed prior to the marriage ceremony under the marriage canopy. The purpose of the *Conditions* is to give the bride and groom access to the laws that existed before the creation of the Universe, when unity and perfection were the essential features of reality, as opposed to the divisiveness and chaos that are the hallmarks of life today.

The various actions performed during the *Conditions* serve to connect the two souls much as they existed when everything was Light. The fathers of the bride and groom break a plate together, signifying the destruction of the *Desire to Receive* in the wedding couple. This action also severs the man and woman from their physical DNA (embodied by their fathers) so that their soul DNA and consciousness can be activated under the canopy. These and other tools are all part of a metaphysical, spiritual technology that operates on the soul level of reality.

For any marriage to truly work, both parties must now commit some portion of their lives to sharing spiritual wisdom and volunteering to improve the lives of others. Both must have a desire to remove the pain, suffering and darkness that afflict all humankind. Unfortunately, 99 percent of all marriages are based on selfish desire, where the man and woman are only worried about their own happiness.

There is nothing wrong with wanting to be happy. The problem is that we don't know how to achieve lasting happiness. The kabbalist understands that life is based on paradoxes. For instance, if we seek happiness for ourselves we receive chaos instead. Yet when we strive to make others happy, *we ourselves* receive happiness. The more we share with others, the more the Light of the Creator is shared with us. That is the secret of happiness. Now you know.

The first place to start sharing is with your spouse. But here's a common problem. When you ask someone why he or she loves another person, this individual responds how wonderful the other person makes him or her feel, how the other person fulfills one's personal needs. But according to Kabbalah, this is *not* true love. Quite the reverse! The person here is telling you all about what he or she is receiving—*not sharing*. Love means giving of yourself and *sharing* without any thought of what you are receiving. It's not about how the other person makes you feel; rather, it's about how you make the other person feel.

The vast majority of marriages, relationships, and partnerships are based upon need, not love, which explains why they are so chaotic.

The key to a fulfilling, passionate marriage is to share unconditionally, to *resist* all forms of receiving. Resistance of desire works like resistance in an electrical circuit. When a filament in a light bulb resists the flow of electrons, the resistance causes the filament to glow. Likewise, when we *resist* receiving and we share instead, our act of resistance causes the Light to pour forth, illuminating both our spouse and *ourselves*! That is how the paradox works; this is how a couple becomes a beacon of Light for others.

The Sabbath Groom (*Shabbat Chatan*)

The first Sabbath immediately after the wedding offers the bride and groom a powerful opportunity. For the first seven days after the wedding, the Vessel of the newly married couple is being built. The Sabbath after the wedding instills the couple's Vessel with all the potential spiritual energy, Light and blessings that they can receive throughout their lives together, like a seed. Just as an apple seed contains within it the entire tree that will grow in the future, the Light received on the couple's first married Sabbath is the seed that contains all the Light necessary for building a loving, fulfilling, and transformative life together. In other words, the entire *tree* that will be the couple's married life together is given to them on this Sabbath.

However, there are two kinds of trees. There is the *Tree of Life*, which is a code name for the perfection that existed prior to Creation, and there is the *Tree of Good and Evil*, which is expressed through our Universe of chaos and order. If we walk the way of the kabbalist and transform ourselves accordingly, our lives become a Tree of Life, a perfected existence overflowing with an unending supply of fruit. But if we walk the path of the material world, governed by ego, our life becomes a Tree of Good and Evil.

Each couple is given the seed, the DNA, to create a perfect Tree of Life existence. When enough people attain this perfected existence, a critical mass will be achieved, and the entire world will be transformed into the Tree of Life Reality, also known as the World of Light.

This first wedding Sabbath is known as the Sabbath of the Groom. In this specific instance, the word *groom* (*Chatan* in Hebrew) does not refer to the husband; it refers to a certain kind of spiritual energy. Kabbalah teaches that there are two kinds of spiritual Light or energy: Inner Light and Surrounding Light. Inner Light refers to the wisdom and blessings that we have inherited as well as what we've already earned. Surrounding Light is the potential spiritual wisdom and Light that we still have not grasped. As we share with others, Surrounding Light enters into us and becomes Inner Light, bringing us greater understanding and increased happiness and joy.

Covering of the Woman's Hair

As we noted earlier, hair channels Light. Hair can be compared to a copper wire that transmits electrical current. A good electrician never leaves wires exposed; they must be insulated in order to safely channel electrical energy to its intended destination. Spiritual Light works the same way. A woman's hair is the conduit that conducts raw energy: pure divine Light. Covering it with a hat, scarf or wig is akin to coating wire in insulation. When a woman covers her head, she ensures that the Light conducted by her hair can only be accessed by her husband, allowing it to manifest blessings, sustenance and wisdom for their entire family.

Single women are not required to cover their hair for they are, at present, only one half of a complete soul. Once married, their souls become whole; a circuit of spiritual energy is generated, and now the woman's hair becomes the spiritual equivalent of a live wire.

Sex

Sexual union between a husband and wife is a profound spiritual tool that can transform not only the lives of the participants but also the entire world. We already discussed sex in the chapter on "Pregnancy"; what follows are some additional insights that will help bring a constant flow of passion, excitement, and sacredness in your sex life.

A Microcosm of Creation

A man and woman in the throes of an orgasm are in the exact same relationship as the Light and Vessel in the original Creation. Sex, when imbued with the right consciousness, embodies the ultimate goal of Creation—union between the Light of the Creator and the souls of humanity. The right consciousness is one of total sharing, in which the male shares for the purpose of imparting pleasure to his partner, and the female receives for the purpose of sharing with her partner.

The Significance of Kissing, Touching, and Foreplay

Foreplay is a vital aspect of lovemaking, according to Kabbalah. As the *Zohar* states in the section of *Pekudei*, 51:652:

> *"There are no kisses of joy and love except when they cling to each other, mouth-to-mouth, spirit-to-spirit, and saturate each other with pleasure and ecstasy."*

During foreplay, a male should devote all his energy to arousing his partner to the highest possible degree. Why? This leads us to a key kabbalistic principle:

The Light of the Creator cannot manifest and express itself without a Receiver.

When a woman is aroused, her sexual desire intensifies and she becomes a true Vessel, a recipient for energy from the

World of Light. The greater a woman's desire becomes, the more room there is for Light to fill her. This is a critically important concept. Kabbalah teaches that when a man and women unite in passionate lovemaking, our physical world and the World of Light *mirror this union.* This is not a metaphor. This is not an analogy. This is a fact.

The sexual arousal of a woman arouses all of physical existence, and expands its ability to draw down divine Light into our World of Darkness. For this reason, the more a man seduces, arouses, and charms a woman—both prior to intercourse and during—the more Light the couple and our dark, chaotic world will receive in turn. As the great medieval Kabbalist Moses ben Nachman put it, *"It is fitting to win her heart with words of charm and seduction and other proper things."*

Abstaining during the Menstrual Cycle (the Practice of *Niddah*)

When a couple makes love with the intent to have a child and the egg is fertilized by the sperm, the menstrual cycle stops, and the woman connects to the energy of Light because now we have:

- male sharing with female
- female sharing with male
- sperm sharing with egg
- mother sharing with child

The womb prepares itself each month to bring forth life and if this does not happen there is no potential for this sharing cycle.

There is no soul to hold the Light of creation and human life. When the menstrual blood is dispelled, this correlates to the shattering of the Cosmic Vessel into sparks of souls mentioned earlier, so we do not want to connect with this energy of separation. Resisting sex during this period keeps the Light switched on.

A woman's body literally takes on a tiny bit of "death" energy when menstrual blood is dispelled and the chance for new life is lost. In the days that follow, the body and soul of the woman are restored, and the body prepares for a new opportunity to bring forth life. Consider this process five days of cleaning house followed by seven days of rebuilding a new Vessel.

According to Kabbalah, you should abstain from sex beginning with the first sign of blood, and lasting for seven days after the time she is free of spotting—usually a twelve-day time frame in total. For those who find the prospect of going twelve days without orgasm daunting, consider this: penguins reach orgasm only once a year. Be happy you're human!

The seven days of abstinence after the woman's period correspond to the seven dimensions, or *Sefirot*, hidden from our view, from which Light flows down into the woman's soul. During this seven-day period a woman's soul is rebuilt, and she is born anew. Consequently, the relationship between husband and wife is also born anew. After this period of abstinence, sex can remind you of what it felt like the very first time. Passions soar!

After the period of abstinence, on the night when sex will take place a woman will prepare herself by bathing for thirty minutes and then immersing herself in a *mikveh*, thirteen times. This preparation serves to literally transform the woman into a new bride for her husband. Immersion in the *mikveh* concludes the menstrual phase and prepares a woman's soul to be a powerful Vessel for the Light of the Creator once more.

Illness

We have discussed how children come into this world, how they are born and how they grow, and how couples can come together to create more children and bring more Light to this world through their relationship. Let us now turn to another responsibility of adulthood, namely the need to confront illness.

Fortunately, Kabbalah offers us powerful healing tools, such as those contained in the section of the *Zohar* known as *Pinchas*. This section of the *Zohar* reveals the underlying cause and true origins of all sicknesses, that of human consciousness. Startlingly, these ancient healing secrets turn out to be *identical* to recent insights emerging from medical science.

In order to uncover these extraordinary secrets, we turn to the *Zohar*.

The Secrets of the *Zohar*

Before we open up the ancient *Zohar* and reveal its insights into health and illness, we must first understand that the term "illness" refers to not just the physcial body; it includes a setback in business, an ailing relationship, and such debilitating emotions as anxiety and depression. In other words, according to the *Zohar*, fixing our financial, marital and mental woes is considered part of the spiritual healing process. It is simply our personal karma that determines whether "disease" strikes the body, the business, the bedroom, or the brain.

Did you know that medical science had no idea that cholesterol levels were related in any way to heart disease until quite recently? It took until the 1970s for scientists to figure out that cholesterol, fat in the blood, and blockages in our arteries were related to heart disease; scientists didn't know that there were two kinds of cholesterol until the 1980s. In 1984, the National Institutes of Health (NIH) published a report titled "Lowering Blood Cholesterol to Prevent Heart Disease," stating that LDL cholesterol, known as "bad" cholesterol, tends to clog blood vessels, and HDL cholesterol, known as "good" cholesterol, tends to scrub vessel walls clean of bad cholesterol.

The NIH report states:

"The LDL particles, when present in excess in the blood, are deposited in the tissues and form a major part of a buildup in the artery wall to form atherosclerotic plaque. Atherosclerosis narrows the channels of the coronary arteries, the vessels that furnish the major blood supply to the heart muscle."

In other words, too much bad cholesterol blocks our arteries, reducing blood flow, which in turn causes heart attacks and certain kinds of strokes.

Then, in the 1990s, scientists also figured out that there are two kinds of fat: good fats and bad fats. Good fats are called omega-3 fatty acids. Thus, we have science telling us that good fats and good cholesterol can help reduce the risk of heart disease, and that bad fat and bad cholesterol can block our arteries and cause heart disease.

The ancient *Zohar*, when commenting upon the Torah section known as *Pinchas*, said the exact same thing two thousand years ago:

> *"... in the body there are pure and impure fatty parts, clean blood without waste matter and blood contaminated with waste matter..."*

> —The *Zohar* Vol. 20, 40:220

According to the *Zohar*, heart disease, brain damage, and death will occur if our bodies contain high levels of the "impure fats."

The *Zohar* goes on to give us another remarkable insight:

> *"From the liver and the appendage emerges the gall, which is the sword of the Angel of Death, from which come bitter drops to kill human beings."*
> —The *Zohar* Vol. 20, 60:364

The *Zohar* says that our negative emotions, most notably anger, rage, and all reactive impulses, manifest in our liver. And medical science has discovered that the liver secretes bile, the primary component of which is cholesterol. Thus, an excess of gall (bile or bitterness) can create illness!

The *Zohar* says our behavior—bitter or kind—determines whether our liver "offers the heart" the pure fats or the impure fats.

The *Zohar* offers dozens of more powerful passages that explain liver function, heart disease, cancer, and other illnesses. What, then, does the *Zohar* say is the origin of all disease?

Our behavior towards others.

There it is. The cause is not our diet. And in the end, it is not really our DNA or our genes. Those are merely the weapons that the negative force uses to inflict judgment upon us—judgment that we arouse through our own ego and intolerance. But who pulled the trigger to activate disease and allow these foods or genes to kill us?

We did.

Here's another way of looking at it. The *Zohar* asks, *Why did a soul choose a body with a specific predisposition to disease in the first place? And why do some genes that cause disease get activated, while others remain dormant?* The kabbalists tell us that our DNA changes throughout our lives based on our behavior. This helps explain why one person who smokes a pack of cigarettes a day can eventually have a heart attack, but another person who smokes two packs a day lives to be 110.

Let's examine this idea further. Imagine that an unknown assailant shoots someone in a dark alley and kills him. The final police report describes how the murder took place—the caliber of the weapon, the number of bullets, the entry wounds, etc. But this information proves to be useless when the killer strikes again, shooting and killing someone else. This time we get another police report with even more information: the shoes the murderer was wearing, the weather at the time of the killing, the family history of the victim. However, a kabbalist is not interested in makes or models or serial numbers. The gun is only a weapon. The bullet is simply a component of that weapon.

Instead, the kabbalist wants to know one thing:

Who pulled the trigger?

Once the police catch the murderer, the root cause of the killings has been neutralized. Weapons cannot kill on their own. All those medical reports about the causes of disease miss the point entirely! They merely describe the various weapons used to kill us, whether they be our genetic inheritance or our greasy pastrami sandwiches.

The *Zohar* also explains that "blockages" can occur in other areas of our lives. Essentially, all of our relationships can get blocked just like an artery in a heart. For instance, when the "artery" of marriage is blocked, love and passion can no longer flow between a husband and wife and the marriage can suffer a heart attack.

Our various business relationships are also arteries, through which the money and deals we make flow. When these vessels are clogged, then good fortune fails to flow to us. Furthermore, if we cheat in business, our bottom line might prosper but we may wind up paying for it with hardening of the arteries and a triple bypass.

All the relationships of the world—between friends, business partners, buyer and seller, brother and sister, husband and wife, parents and children, one nation and another—are spiritual arteries that can become blocked when humans behave with intolerance toward one another. Each time you interact with someone in your life, no matter who it is, you are affecting the channels in your life and in the world. If your behavior in these relationships is governed by reactive impulses and self-interest, you will create a fatty deposit. If these blockages continue to grow and are left unchecked, "dis-ease" sets in. This can manifest as poverty, war, divorce, kids on drugs, dysfunctional families, global terrorism—or a good old-fashioned heart attack!

Ultimately, it is our behavior that determines whether we enjoy good health or succumb to disease.

Take a moment now to quiet your mind. Open your heart. Let go of all your doubts, just for a moment. Let go of all your preconceived notions about life and death, healing and medicine, and all the social conditioning that affects your life. Be still.

How do we cure ourselves of disease? The first step is accountability: to be prepared to take charge of our lives and to accept responsibility for them. And this is, without a doubt, the most difficult step of all to take. We must lose the victim mindset and realize that something we did, in this life or in a past life, caused the situation we find ourselves in. Once we can truly accept responsibility—100 percent—then, and only then, will the tools of Kabbalah arouse the Light of the Creator so that we can be healed!

Some of these powerful healing tools include:

- Hearing the Torah Reading every Saturday, regardless of your faith or background (especially the section known as *Pinchas*).
- *Zohar* meditation/scanning.
- Attending the Third Meal connection on the Sabbath (Kabbalists say this boosts the immune system in the most powerful way possible).
- Drinking Kabbalah Water (to nurture the cells of our body, boost the immune system, and cleanse spiritual blockages).
- Give to charity. According to the *Zohar*, charity—especially when giving is uncomfortable—can save us from death.

Visiting the Sick

A critical aspect of spiritual growth and of maintaining an open connection with the World of Light is taking time to visit the sick. According to the *Zohar*, each individual who visits a sick individual removes one-sixtieth of that person's ailment. Imagine how good it would be for a sick person if sixty spiritually minded people took the time to visit. He or she would be healed!

Visiting the sick can become even more powerful through meditating on various Names of God during your visit.

Yud, Lamed, Yud יִלִי

While meditating on this Name of God, we take the right hand of the ailing person in our right hand giving this individual the power to rise out of his or her despair. When illness strikes, we often feel like victims. This Name of God literally lifts us up out of our hopeless state of mind, giving us courage, energy, strength, and a sense of accountability and control over our situation, allowing us to start healing ourselves at the seed level, at the level of consciousness.

Mem, Hei, Shin מ ה שׁ

This sequence consists of the same letters that form the name Moses. It imparts pure healing power to the individual.

Yud, Yud, Yud, Yud יי יי

This is one of the most powerful Names of God for healing. Visualize the letters over the ailing person's head and bathe him or her in green light, followed by blue light, and then concluding with pure white light.

Death

Every soul comes into this world to find ultimate happiness. To make this a worthwhile challenge so that we become the actual *creators* of our happiness, the soul wears a costume called the ego. It not only conceals your true identity from others, but it hides your true self from you! According to Kabbalah, every person is given an average of seventy years to remove the ego, conquer selfishness, and discover the truth about life. This is what the path of spirituality and Kabbalah are all about. Every time we listen to our ego, every time we react and behave with intolerance, anger, fear, selfishness or resentment, a curtain is placed over the Light that shines within us. When those curtains become dense enough, the Light is finally blocked out completely, and the body loses contact with the soul, the true you—which leads to death. The soul now ascends into the spiritual world and awaits a new body to try to win the Game of Life once again.

Death also serves as a cleansing agent. It's a purifier that removes all the curtains we have built up. When we finally remove the ego from our being once and for all, there will be no curtains left to dim the Light of our soul, and the body and soul will live forever. We will have achieved immortality. It is only the human ego that makes us doubtful. Once the ego is banished, the certainty of immortality ignites within our consciousness.

Another way to understand death is through the concept of space. According to Kabbalah there is no *Angel of Death*, only an *Angel of Space*. According to physics, everything that exists is made of matter and energy, and two laws of physics—the Law of Conservation of Matter, and the Law of Conservation of Energy—state that matter and energy can never be destroyed. They can be rearranged, yes, sometimes quite radically, but they cannot be completely removed. Every bit of matter and energy that has ever existed in the universe *still exists*. In other words, matter and energy are *immortal*. Matter and energy never die.

You and I are made up of matter and energy, as are the vegetable kingdom and the animal kingdom. So if matter and energy live forever, why do we die? Because the matter and energy that constitute our beings rearrange themselves. The configuration of atoms and molecules and chemical reactions that produces an individual simply stops working together. Deadly space opens up between the body's components. Kabbalah says this space is created through selfish consciousness and behavior. When we create space between ourselves and other people (in accord with the ego), space is injected into the structures and processes of our body. This is why we die.

Once space reaches a critical mass, *death* occurs. The specific form it takes is secondary; the ego, and the space that it creates, underlie every cause of death. Once death occurs, the matter and energy that used to constitute your body circulate back into the environment and wait for another opportunity to try once more to complete the transformation of the ego. The kabbalists teach that some of the components of the original body will seek out certain other human bodies or even animals or inanimate matter for karmic reasons, in order to complete the process of transformation.

A certain amount of "space" consciousness—that is, death consciousness—already exists in our world. The moment we are born, we have already begun the long process of dying. However, once enough people in our world transform their consciousness from one of receiving into one of unconditional sharing, the space in our world and in our bodies will shrink and disappear. When space (selfishness and receiving behavior) is removed from our consciousness, death will be removed from the world. That is our ultimate destiny.

Seven Days of Mourning

When an individual passes on, his direct relatives (siblings, children, parents or spouse) sit in mourning for seven days. Contrary to popular to belief, the mourners are not there to mourn, but rather to celebrate the person's life and spiritual achievements and assist the soul in its elevation to a higher dimension.

During the seven days of mourning which correspond to the lower seven spiritual dimensions (*Sefirot*), the soul of the departed individual travels back and forth from the grave to the house as it tries to break the bonds of the physical reality.

The process of death can be either easy or painful, depending upon the spiritual level achieved by the departed. According to the *Zohar*, if a person completes his or her transformation, overcoming the ego during the course of a lifetime, the person leaves this world through what is known as *The Kiss*. This transition from physical reality to true reality is painless, seamless and filled with ecstasy.

On the other hand, if a person lived a life of extreme self-indulgence, the process of death can be difficult because such a life has strengthened the ego. A strong ego will cling to physical reality after death, making it that much more difficult for the soul to break free. The mourners' prayers, meditations, and support will help ease the soul's transition from this world to the next.

In the house of the departed person, it is suggested that all mirrors be covered. This is because when a person dies, the soul, at first, does not know it is dead. So when it travels to the house from the grave, and happens to pass an uncovered mirror, it will see itself and experience tremendous pain upon being confronted by the fact of its death.

Family and friends often send meals to the immediate family of the departed. The purpose behind these meals is both to help elevate the soul of the departed as well as assist those closely involved in the dying process or death to remove any influence of "death" that they may have experienced.

After seven days of mourning, one part of the soul (*Neshama*) leaves the physical reality. Thirty days after death, another aspect of the soul (*Ruach*) is elevated. After approximately eleven months has passed, the final part of the soul (*Nefesh*) ascends.

Mourners recite the ancient prayer-connection knows as the *Kaddish* every day for eleven months after the passing of an individual, and on the death anniversary each year. Great misunderstanding surrounds this ancient practice. Traditionally, the *Kaddish* was thought of as a mourner's prayer to help those in mourning deal with their grief. On the contrary, the *Kaddish* is intended to help the soul of the departed ascend to higher levels of spiritual reality. In addition, recitation of this prayer banishes a portion of the Angel of Death (Angel of Space) from this physical reality, and thus, helps to hasten the arrival of immortality.

The Cemetery

The energy found in a cemetery is not usually very positive, for cemeteries are filled with soulless bodies. Because the energy of a body without a soul is pure selfish *Desire to Receive*, which creates separation from the Light, the energy of a cemetery corresponds to the force of death.

According to the kabbalistic sages, children should not attend a funeral at a cemetery if they have not yet had their *Bar/Batmitzvah*, because they are more vulnerable to the negative energy that permeates a graveyard. They still lack the ability to share through the power of free will, and thus, do not have the added protection that sharing offers us as adults.

Also, pregnant women and menstruating women should not visit a cemetery. A fetus is in the same position as a child before his or her *Bar/Batmitzvah*, and a woman experiencing her monthly flow becomes more vulnerable to negativity during that time.

Furthermore, a man should not look into a woman's eyes when in a cemetery. Women, spiritually speaking, are stronger and purer than men, so they can withstand greater exposure to negative energy. Men, being on a lower level in terms of spiritual strength, are more spiritually vulnerable, and thus, should not make eye contact with a woman until after leaving the cemetery, for negative energy is passed through the eyes.

Washing the Hands after Visiting a Cemetery

According to Kabbalah, negative energy always clings to the hands. For this reason, we always wash immediately upon leaving a cemetery. When washing, we pour water over each hand three times (starting with the right hand), and alternating from one hand to the next after each pour.

The Graves of the Righteous Kabbalists

A kabbalist or righteous individual is one who has completely transformed his or her *Desire to Receive* (ego) into unconditional sharing and love. Therefore, when a truly righteous person chooses to leave this world, his or her body does not decompose. The body of such a person is a pure channel for sharing, and therefore, there is no negativity attached to it. The gravesite of a righteous soul also becomes a gateway into the hidden World of Light, the 99 Percent Reality. Anyone can visit the gravesite of a righteous soul in order to tap into their energy and connect to the hidden dimensions of Light that lie beyond this physical reality.

Death Anniversary Candle

Often the simplest actions contain the most powerful effects. When someone passes on, mourners light a memorial or anniversary candle in the name of the individual. The candle, according to Kabbalah, is literally the physical manifestation of a soul. The candle lit every year on the date of the individual's passing connects us directly to the soul of the person. There are many spiritual levels in the next world, each one offering greater joy and fulfillment, and the candle helps the soul continue its ascent to and through these levels. These candles are also lit at various times throughout the year when the cosmos opens up and there is a window into the spiritual reality, including such holidays as *Yom Kippur*, *Passover*, *Shavuot* and *Simchat Torah*.

Another important aspect the sages teach is that because all candlelight connects to souls, we never blow out candles but rather use another means to extinguish them if it is absolutely necessary.

part two

a day in
the life

The Semantics of Prayer: God is the Noun, Humankind the Verb

God does not answer our prayers. Rather, God is the answer to our prayers. From the Kabbalistic perspective, God is more noun than verb. If God answered our prayers, God would be a verb, taking action, getting involved. Instead, *we* are the verb. We need to take action in order to connect with God and draw the Light of the Creator to our lives.

We have had this backwards for two thousand years, which is why our prayers have gone unanswered for so long. We keep waiting for an answer from God, but God cannot answer. God just *is*.

So how do we connect to God?

Transformation. Each time we resist our ego—our self-centered nature that wants to react, scream, cheat, yell, worry and abuse—we connect our soul to God. However, when our buttons are pushed, when some annoying individual incites us to anger, there's almost no way to prevent a reflexive response. So God came up with an idea, a way to help us out. He gave us a technology that we mistakenly called *prayer*.

The kabbalist who prays is not offering a plea, or making a request. The words and letters that compose a prayer literally link our soul to unseen spiritual dimensions from which we summon spiritual help to rise above our ego, our reactive nature, and all the nasty character traits that keep us from connecting to the Light of the Creator.

Prayer is a technology. It is a tool of transformation that enables us to answer our own prayers by connecting to the infinite, divine force of Energy found in the World of Light.

The *Zohar* tells us that if there is a justified decree of death on somebody's life, prayer with the correct consciousness can annul that decree. When we activate the power of prayer (not God) we become co-Creators of our destiny and happiness.

It is up to us to ignite the power of prayer by investing effort, which pretty much means becoming accountable and respon- sible for all the chaos that we encounter. We cannot pray for help as victims of circumstance, or a fatality as a result of some dangerous situation or evil person. Any evil person who harms us is a result of an opening that we created at some point in our past—either in this life or in a previous one.

The moment we accept this difficult truth, our prayers are jump-started. The technology of prayer will now connect us to the Light, but it is our effort that sets it all in motion. This sub- tle truth is illustrated by an old Kabbalistic parable.

> *There was once a man who wanted to please the Creator as much as he could. He prayed day and night, until finally a Voice spoke from the unseen spiritual world and said to him, "I want you to go and push a stone."*
>
> *The man woke up the next morning full of enthu- siasm. He ran out and found a huge boulder down the road from his home. Immediately, he began pushing it. But nothing happened. The*

next morning he woke up and pushed the boulder again. Still nothing happened. This man woke up every morning for three months straight and diligently pushed the boulder with all his might. Yet nothing ever happened. With each failed attempt, the man became more upset by his inability to move the boulder even a single centimeter.

Finally, when the fourth month arrived, the man said to himself, "The heck with this. That darn boulder isn't going anywhere, and I don't understand what this whole thing is about."

Then the man had another dream in which he spoke to the Voice from Heaven saying, "I don't know what You want from me. I tried everything You said, and nothing's happened."

The Creator replied, "Why did you stop?"

The man answered, "Because nothing happened."

God said, "What do you mean, nothing happened? Look at you! Look how strong you are, how determined and focused you are. Look how powerful your muscles are. You are no longer the person you were when you started to push the stone. You have changed. That's what happened. And besides, I didn't tell you to move the stone; I told you to push the stone. I'll move the stone when it's time."

Prayers: Three Times a Day

We pray (connect) to the unseen Light-filled dimensions three times a day. As noted earlier, the Three Column System is the underlying reason behind the tripartite aspect of things we see repeated again and again in the world around us. The morning prayer (*Shacharit*) connects to the Right Column Energy (+), arousing Light for the entire day. The energy awakened by this morning connection arouses the spiritual force known as *mercy*, which helps keep chaos and judgment from our lives. A second connection (*Mincha*)—Left Column Energy (-)—is made by praying in the late afternoon, as the sun is setting. This connection helps to quiet judgments. And a third connection (*Arvit*) which is a connection to Central Column Energy (neutral) is made by praying in the late evening, after the sun has set.

According to the *Zohar*, the evening connection has the power to literally burn away blockages, those within our arteries and those that choke off relationships between people, family, faiths, and nations. The key to activating this power is to recognize and offer up as a sacrifice the *fat* within our own consciousness—namely, the ego. When we recite and perform the evening prayer, we should review our day, recalling as many of our nasty, egocentric moments as possible. The harder it is for us to admit our self-centered behavior, the more successful our connection.

Women are not required to make the daily prayer-connections, for they are on a higher spiritual level and serve a different metaphysical function in the overall scheme of things. Men descend from the original Supernal Male or Right Column;

thus, they are responsible for generating a flow of positive Light into this reality. Women, being from the Supernal Female or Left Column, manifest this Light in their daily lives.

This situation is similar to the relationship between the sun and Earth. The sun emits rays that fall upon the Earth. The Earth's job is to take that sunlight and create life, which it does through photosynthesis and other natural processes. When a man makes a connection to the spiritual world three times a day, he is playing the role of the sun, igniting a flow of Light and energy that will fall upon his family and this Earth. Women use this Light to bring forth spiritual life for the family and the world, just as the earth brings forth water, plant life, and other things necessary for life on Earth.

For more details about the actual prayer connections, see the *Kabbalistic Daily Prayer Book*.

Minyan: The Power of Ten

In the ideal scenario, the morning, afternoon and evening prayer-connections involve ten men praying together. This arrangement awakens unimaginable power, not only for the individuals making the connection but also for the entire city in which the prayer-connections are taking place. Kabbalah tells us that true reality exists in ten dimensions. This is why we have ten fingers and ten toes, and why we conduct mathematics in base ten. So if ten men are present during a prayer-connection, each man will automatically connect to a different dimension, thereby unifying the entire reality. This unification of the ten dimensions is like connecting ten pipes so that energy can flow, uninterrupted, from the World of Light to our World of Darkness.

Hebrew and Aramaic Connections

All languages are heard by God. All prayers, regardless of language, ascend into the spiritual worlds above. However, God gave humankind two special languages that have the unique power to reach the highest heights and generate the most significant and profound spiritual effects. These two languages are Hebrew and Aramaic.

The biggest misconception concerning both languages is that they belong to the nation of Israel. This is not the case. Hebrew and Aramaic are universal, and they belong to all of humankind.

Both Aramaic and Hebrew are written in the Hebrew alphabet, which works exactly like the atomic alphabet. We know that the entire world, from apples to zebras, is made up of atoms, which bond in different ways to produce different forms of matter, the way letters bond to create different words. Hebrew letters, however, do not just construct words. They also construct the metaphysical reality of the thing that the word represents. For instance, the letters that create the Hebrew word for "Light" are not being used to create a word that *describes* something. Rather, these letters are the building blocks of Light *itself*. The letters that spell the word "mercy" are not merely symbols to describe a concept. The letters activate the actual spiritual force of *mercy*.

By making a prayer-connection in Hebrew and Aramaic, you are working with the very DNA of Creation. This is spiritual nanotechnology. In recognition of this great power, the kabbalists prescribed meditations and connections using Aramaic as a way to jump-start our transformation each day, allowing us to take quantum leaps forward in our effort to rid the world of pain and suffering.

Scanning the *Zohar*

Kabbalists throughout history tell us that reading or visually scanning the text of the *Zohar* is the most powerful way to infuse our lives and this world with Divine Energy.

Consider the advice of various kabbalists throughout history:

> *"Reading the* Zohar *is good for the soul, even if wrong and full of mistakes."*
>
> —Rabbi David Azulai (1724–1806)

> *"He who studies the* Zohar, *even when he doesn't understand what comes out of his mouth, God rectifies his words . . . And even when he . . . does not know how to read, even with all this, his reward will be double."*
>
> —Introduction to the *Zohar* printed in the eighteenth century

"One who does not merit understanding the Zohar, should nevertheless learn, because the language of the Zohar purifies the soul."

—Rav Meir Papirash

"The study of Zohar is very lofty, purifying and sanctifying. Read it regularly even if you do not understand the text. Our sages compare this to a baby who is learning to speak. His parents derive great pleasure from his efforts even if he does not understand what he is saying. God similarly derives pleasure when a person reads the holy texts, even if he does not fully comprehend them."

—Kabbalist Rav Eliezer Papo

Why would this be? Why would reading or even just gazing at letters, sentences and paragraphs in a book result in such an infusion of power and energy? The *Zohar* in Volume 16:94 says that if a person studies the spiritual secrets of the Torah (*Zohar*), and he has no teacher, and he cannot understand what he reads, but he nevertheless strives to connect to this wisdom out of love and desire, then "every word will ascend on high," and the Creator "will rejoice in each word that he stumbles over."

The lesson is deeply profound: Our lack of knowledge, our inability to read and grasp the Aramaic text of the *Zohar*, and our great distance from the Light are the very factors that enable us to draw closer to the Light—closer than the most righteous sage, if our love and desire burn brightly. *Our weakness is actually our greatest strength!*

So instead of being discouraged over our lack of knowledge, and instead of being frustrated by our inability to read Aramaic, we should know with total conviction that as a result of making this loving effort to scan the *Zohar*, we will be "ravished with Love" by the Creator. The more effort, trust and certainty we inject into our use of these tools, the more powerful they become.

It is true that someone who is well versed in Aramaic, someone who is wise, scholarly, and deeply learned in biblical wisdom, will find it easier to read and grasp the wisdom of the *Zohar*. But such a person would experience little character change as a result of reading the *Zohar* because he or she would not be putting much effort into one's actions—and it's all about the effort.

The Promise of the *Zohar*

The most prolific kabbalist, not only of the twentieth century but in all of history, is the great Rav Yehuda Ashlag (1885–1954), who founded The Kabbalah Centre in 1922. Each night Rav Ashlag (like all the great kabbalists before him) would rise in the middle of the night to study the *Zohar*. Rav Ashlag said that the wonderful benefits and great rewards deriving from this action had nothing to do with the amount of learning and wisdom acquired. This eminent kabbalist said it was the difficult act of climbing out of bed that ignited the Light; it was all about effort. Those who put forth the effort to connect to the *Zohar* will be protected during times of judgment as if they were on the ark of Noah, and at the end of their trials, they will be showered with blessings and good fortune. This is the promise of the *Zohar*.

My father's teacher, Rav Brandwein, told the Rav during their years of studying together that the Rav should feel confident in promising anything to anyone if they supported the printing and distribution of the *Zohar*, such is the awesome power and monumental importance of the *Zohar* in this world.

You are probably familiar with the story of Moses, Mount Sinai, and the Tablets containing the so-called Ten Commandments. The ancient kabbalists tell us that what really took place on Sinai thirty-four centuries ago was a state of revelation that produced immortality and paradise on Earth. Every man, woman, and child attained immortality and experienced the unimaginable joy and bliss associated with the arrival of the Messiah and the Garden of Eden on Earth. This blissful state was created through the revelation of *Light*, a profound infusion of a spiritual force that literally eradicated death and darkness from the planet.

But then something went wrong. The Israelites, we're told, built a golden calf while Moses was on Sinai receiving the Tablets. The building of the golden calf is actually a code for the fact that the Israelites were not yet willing to sacrifice their egos. In Kabbalah, we learn that during one's lifetime, either the ego dies or the body dies. When the ego (the Adversary) is completely banished from our being, the body and soul will live forever.

The Israelites preferred to keep the ego alive. Consequently, the state of immortality for the body and soul suddenly ended, and the Light that gave rise to this temporary state of paradise was hidden away. Where was this glorious Light hidden? Where did immortality go? That, as they say, is the million-dollar question.

The answer is that after Moses smashed the first set of Tablets in anger at the Israelites' disobedience, a second set of Tablets was created out of sapphire. Moses received these second Tablets directly from God in a cave on Mount Sinai.

Within these Tablets was infused all the Light and energy that has the power necessary to reactivate immortality on planet Earth. Kabbalah refers to this energy by the Hebrew term, *Or haGanuz* (*The Hidden Light*).

Now we must face an even more haunting and compelling question: where are those second Tablets?

The Splendor Upon Moses' Face

The Torah says that when the Israelites built the golden calf, Moses came down from the mountain and smashed the original two Tablets as a result of this great sin. The destruction of the Tablets disconnected the world from immortality. As we've just learned, Moses then went back up the mountain to receive a second set of Tablets, made of sapphire. The Torah says that when Moses returned with the second set of Tablets, his face was radiating intense Light.

In his commentary on this episode, the word that eleventh-century Spanish Kabbalist Abraham Ibn Ezra uses to describe the Light that shone from the face of Moses is *Zohar*. Ibn Ezra was not the only one. The great thirteenth-century astronomer, astrologer, mathematician, and biblical commentator Rav Levi ben Gershom, known as Gersonides, also uses the word *Zohar* to describe the energy emanating from the face of Moses.

Another great fifteenth-century sage, Kabbalist Rav Don Isaac Abarbanel, also uses the word *Zohar* a number of times when providing astute commentary on the Light that shone from Moses' face, and he says this is a very deep secret.

The Torah tells us that Moses was forced to wear a veil to conceal the Light that Ezra, Gersonides, and Don Isaac identified as *Zohar*.

Rashi (Rav Solomon ben Isaac), perhaps the greatest of all medieval biblical commentators, revealed a staggering secret with regard to this peculiar veil. The entire Bible is written in the language of Hebrew. Yet, Rashi pointed out that the actual word used in the Torah for the veil (*masveh*) that Moses wore in the Story of *Ki Tisa*, is in fact, *Aramaic*, not Hebrew. Here we have discovered a profound secret and clear reference to the greatest source of kabbalistic wisdom, the book of the *Zohar*, a book that was written in the language of *Aramaic*. All the kabbalists of history have acknowledged the Aramaic *Zohar* to be as the *veil* that conceals the Hidden Light (the *Or haGanuz*), which is nothing less than the Light of Immortality.

The Revelation of the *Zohar*

This means that the dissemination of the *Zohar* into our world is literally the revelation and restoration of the Light of Immortality. Studying the text of the *Zohar* is equivalent to *unveiling* the Light of Immortality. Meditating on the text, or even just visually scanning the words, is an act of replenishing the hidden Light of Immortality. This is why the great kabbalists of history tell us to read or scan the *Zohar*, even if we do not understand a single word of it. Encoded into every letter, word, and verse of the Aramaic text of the *Zohar* is the mind-blowing spiritual force and Light that produced immortality on Earth thirty-four centuries ago.

According to the kabbalists, the *Zohar* should be scanned every day for at least five minutes. It is also beneficial to study its texts after midnight, alone or with a teacher or friends. Each time we meditate upon or study the *Zohar*'s text, we restore a portion of the Light that was lost on Mount Sinai. The more *Zohars* that circulate in the world, and the more people who scan their texts, the more quickly we will banish darkness and death from this world.

The 42-Letter Name of God (Prayer of the Kabbalist)

Each day, the kabbalists recite what is known as the *42-Letter Name of God (Ana Beko'ach)*. This powerful sequence of letters gives us the ability to rise above all the negative influences that surround us each day. Seven stanzas in this recitation correspond to the seven days of the week, and special daily meditations correspond to what is known as the *Angels of the Day*. Do not mistakenly think of angels as stereotypical little cherubs with wings. Angels are authentic spiritual influences and metaphysical forces we can tap into as a way of infusing our day with positive energy and keeping negative energy at bay.

We use the Angels of the Day and the seven stanzas to give us genuine control over our lives. Without these connections, we are vulnerable to all of the forces of chaos that swirl around us. For comprehensive insights into these powerful daily connections, see my book *The Prayer of the Kabbalist: The 42-Letter Name of God*.

The Return of the Soul (*Modeh Ani*)

During sleep, the soul ascends into the higher dimensions to recharge by receiving infusions of Divine Energy. This is the purpose of sleep. When we wake, there is a prayer that kabbalists recite the moment we open our eyes to ensure that our soul completely return to our body. By doing so, we express appreciation for being given a new day in which we can continue our transformation toward the ultimate goal of paradise on earth. The moment we wake, we recite the following:

(מוֹדָה :Women say)　　מוֹדֶה
Modah　　　　　　　Modeh

שֶׁהֶחֱזַרְתָּ　וְקַיָּם　חַי　מֶלֶךְ　לְפָנֶיךָ　אֲנִי
Shehechezarta　vekayam　chai　melech　lefanecha　ani

בִּי　נִשְׁמָתִי　בְּחֶמְלָה.　רַבָּה　אֱמוּנָתֶךָ:
bi　nishmati　b'chemlah　rab'bah　emonatecha

Washing of the Hands

Each morning upon rising, the kabbalist washes his hands using a two-handed cup or pitcher, pouring water over each hand three times; pouring first over the right hand and then alternating from one to the other for a total of six pours. The reason we alternate hands is because the negative forces jump from one hand to the other as the water strikes our hands.

When we alternate three times, we chase the negative entities from hand to hand until they finally fall away.

Kabbalistically speaking, the energy of sleep is equivalent to one-sixtieth of death. During the night, negative forces cling to our hands and fingers. When we wash, we dissolve all negative influences from our hands.

The kabbalist also washes prior to breaking bread. Bread is a powerful conductor of spiritual energy, so before we eat it we need to resist the *Desire to Receive* that is associated with the hands, and to remove all negative influences from our fingers.

Blessings Before Food

Blessing is a confusing word. Its connotations are religious, suggesting that we are praising or thanking God for the food we eat. However, the truth is that God does not need or want our thanks. Nor did we come into this world to sing God's praises; we came here to become the Cause and creator of our own joy, happiness and Light. To give us this opportunity, the Light (paradise) was hidden away. Our job is to find it. When we do, we become responsible for bringing it to all the people of the world. This is how we become the creators of our own happiness: we have to take actions to ignite Light, positive energy and blessings in our lives.

The point is that blessings are dependent upon us, not upon God. Never forget: we asked God for this opportunity. Instead of having paradise and eternal happiness given to us as a charitable handout, we wanted to emulate the Creator and create this happiness on our own. So the Light was hidden. This is why we find ourselves in a dark world where lasting happiness, truth and joy are hard to find. But when we do find it, we have become responsible for making it available to ourselves and others, and that experience provides the greatest fulfillment we could ever have.

The Light is hidden in many forms. Relationships. Sex. Food. Money. Children. Nature. Music. Creativity. These are just some of the garments that conceal the original Light, which is why we love all these treasures so much. However, there is a particular way to *reveal* the hidden spark of Light in all of the above items; a way that allows us to receive as much of the Divine Energy as possible. Consider the case of food. If we simply eat food without reciting the blessing, the spark of Light inside the food remains dormant and inactive; all we receive from the food is nutrition, which only constitutes one percent of the food's energy. But when we recite blessings over the food we ignite the Divine spark within it, enabling us to receive both the one percent of its energy that nourishes our bodies and the 99 percent of its energy that feeds our souls.

By reciting the blessing, *we* become the Cause of the Light's revelation in the food. Now the food not only provides nutrition but also healing, wellness and spiritual contentment. According to sixteenth-century Kabbalist Rav Isaac Luria (the Ari), a body only filled with nutrients inevitably becomes dark and spiritually weighted down. Moreover, food that is eaten without its Light being released through blessing will feed the negative forces that dwell within the body as a result of selfish, reactive behavior. When we bless the food, we ignite the Light, and any negative forces within us are deprived of nourishment.

Kosher

The world is made up of three forces: positive, negative, and neutral (resistance). This is the Three Column System we spoke of earlier. As you know, a light bulb must have a negative pole, a positive pole, and a filament in order to give light. The concept of kosher food works the same way. The idea is to create a circuit of energy so that spiritual forces of Light shine from our food the same way light shines from a light bulb.

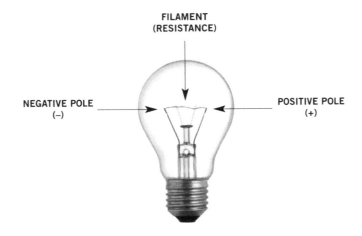

FILAMENT (RESISTANCE)

NEGATIVE POLE (–)

POSITIVE POLE (+)

In kosher households, milk and meat are never mixed. Milk corresponds to the positive pole in a light bulb. Milk is white, like white sunlight, which is whole, containing all the colors of the spectrum. Milk is intended for the purpose of sharing and giving life, feeding the young. Milk has continuity; it never spoils, instead being used for yogurt or cheeses. Dairy foods are absorbed by the body quickly, usually within thirty minutes. All these characteristics categorize milk as positive sharing energy.

Meat, on the other hand, is red, the lowest frequency on the color spectrum. It comes from an animal that has been slaughtered, which is the opposite of sharing life. Meat takes five to six hours to digest, indicating meat's strong desire to receive not to share. Meat is considered to be from the Left Column, possessed of negative energy.

When foods imbued with these two forces connect in the body, they create a spiritual short-circuit. When we create a resistance to ingest milk and meat at the same time, we create the filament that allows the spiritual Light to shine in our body and soul. If kabbalists eat meat, they wait six hours before ingesting a dairy product, to prevent a direct connection between positive and negative. If dairy is ingested first the waiting period is within thirty minutes, since dairy is absorbed quickly into the body.

We do not eat pork, because pork originates from the Two Column System, (whereas cattle stems from the Three Column System). For instance, a cow has a split hoof (Two Columns) and chews its own cud, which is an act of resistance (Third Column), in that instead of ingesting food immediately, the cow resists and chews the food again before fully ingesting it. A pig has a split hoof but does not chew its cud; thus, the pig is missing the Third Column (resistance). Similar principles explain why the kabbalist also refrains from eating shellfish, bottom-feeders in the ocean, crustaceans and horsemeat. All the kosher laws can be traced back to the Three Column System; Kosher is a technology for ensuring that our diet creates spiritual balance and a free flow of energy.

For meat, the koshering process involves the method used to slaughter an animal. Kabbalists believe that an aspect of a person's soul might reincarnate into an animal for a karmic purpose, and koshering is a way to remove reincarnated negativity from an animal's blood. When the meat from the animal is koshered, every drop of blood is removed so that no trace of a reincarnated soul remains in the animal. Also, the animal feels no pain when slaughtered according to kosher procedures. If an animal feels pain during slaughtering, the negativity associated with pain engulfs the entire animal, and this negativity is transferred to the person who ingests its meat. Moreover, if an animal is koshered, the person who eats the animal actually elevates all the sparks of soul that reside inside the animal.

Kabbalah Water

More than three hundred years ago, the great eighteenth-century Italian Kabbalist Moses Hayim Luzzatto (the *Ramchal*) and the renowned nineteenth-century Kabbalist Joseph Hayim of Baghdad said that at the End of Days a special water will transform people and the world. Simply by drinking it, this water would assist an individual's transformation. They cited other kabbalistic sources dating back thousands of years, and the Torah, as the authority behind this statement.

Water was always destined to play an important role in the elevation of humankind and the world. The kabbalists possessed special formulae, based upon sacred Divine Names of God, to imbue water with spiritual energy. Water is the substance on Earth that most closely embodies the qualities of the Light of the Creator. Water is really a form of liquid Light. In ancient times, the waters of the Earth possessed inherent healing qualities, and this is why the biblical figures of history lived for hundreds of years. Water in those days could not cause harm; there were no drownings or destructive floods. After the biblical flood during the time of Noah, the waters of the Earth became corrupted, and water evolved a dual nature of both mercy and judgment. The ancient kabbalists said that when the time of our Redemption came, the Holy Names of God and other kabbalistic technologies would be used to restore water to its original pristine state.

Ever since the time of Noah, only kabbalists have known how to tap into the original pristine waters. For instance, kabbalists know of a precise location in the Sea of Galilee where Miriam's Well can be found. Miriam was the sister of Moses. Thanks to her merit, a well of water accompanied the Israelites while they journeyed through the desert. Miriam's Well refers to both the primordial waters of Earth and to the spiritual power and energy of the 99 Percent Reality, since water is merely a reflection of this Light.

In the sixteenth century, the great Kabbalist Isaac Luria took his beloved disciple and successor, Chaim Vital, into the middle of the lake so that his student could drink from Miriam's Well. This allowed Haim Vital to diminish his ego and, in turn, strengthen his soul so he could grasp the great secrets of Kabbalah that Rav Luria was going to impart to him.

Kabbalah Water undergoes a number of precisely ordered kabbalistic procedures according to the instructions of Kabbalist Isaac Luria and the teachings of the *Zohar*. Certain springs throughout the world that contain specific kinds of surrounding vegetation and that receive specific amounts of consecutive days of rainfall are required for the creation of Kabbalah Water.

The *Zohar* and the kabbalists were quite specific regarding the kinds of wells and springs that could be used. All the water gathered today from these special places is then treated with various ancient meditations and blessings; these shift the water's molecular structure by controlling the very conscious-ness of the water, causing it to become a powerful medium for transferring the Light of the Creator into our bodies and souls.

The Red String

"A person possessed of an evil eye carries with him the eye of the destroying negative force; hence such a person is called a 'destroyer of the world.' People should be on their guard against such a person and not come near them so that they should not be injured by them!"

—The Zohar

The Red String is a powerful tool that wards off and intercepts all the negative influences transmitted by an evil eye. "Evil Eye" refers to any jealous stare, envious glance or hateful look directed our way. It does not matter whether this look of ill will is intentional or not; a negative influence still radiates from the eyes of the individual.

The Red String comes from Israel, where it is wrapped around the tomb of Rachel, the great matriarch of the Bible. It is said that Rachel cries tears for her children every day to protect us from destruction. Wrapping the string around Rachel's Tomb infuses the wool of the string with a proactive power that acts like a vaccination against the metaphysical viruses that attack us each day. Make no mistake: even the smallest of negative stares affects our body, spiritually and physically.

The Red String is worn on the left wrist, and fastened by seven knots that correspond to the seven *Sefirot* (dimensions) that influence our physical reality. There is also an ancient sequence of words that is recited by the person who ties the string to your wrist. To the kabbalist, the Red String is so important that he or she ties it onto the wrist of a newborn baby within moments of the child's birth. To learn more details about the Red String, you might want to read *The Red String Book.*

Fringes and Head Coverings (*Tzitzit, Talit, Kippa*)

As we've seen, the Light of the Creator corresponds to the positive flow of energy, similar to the positive pole in a light bulb. The human brain and hair correspond to the negative pole in a light bulb. The head covering (*Yarmulke* or *Kippa*) acts as the filament that creates resistance so that spiritual Light will shine throughout our being. The kabbalist always covers his head, in order to create a circuit of energy.

During prayer-connections, a married man will wear a prayer shawl with fringes, or *Talit.* The prayer shawl has four corners that act as transmitters to broadcast the spiritual Light summoned by the individual to the four corners of the Earth. Kabbalistcally, the Light drawn by the *Talit* is known as Surrounding Light (*Or Makif*); and this broadcast of Light instills our entire physical reality with energy on a quantum level, affecting the entire world and all its people simultaneously.

A kabbalist also wears underneath garments or shirts (*Tzitzit*) with fringes that are specifically designed to act as a metaphysical antenna that draw the Light of protection to us. The Light drawn is known by the kabbalists as Inner Light (*Or Penimi*). The energy force that is generated by this garment motivates and pushes us, consciously and subconsciously, to achieve greater spiritual heights and to evolve ever further.

The *Tzitzit* has another purpose: it conjures up our hidden memories of the Endless World, the true Light that can bring us never-ending happiness, as opposed to the temporary, immediate gratifications associated with self-interest and the physical world. We used to know about this World of Light, but that memory is now hidden behind the curtain that is the Adversary and ego. Ego prevents us from seeing our true selves and our true purpose in life. The *Tzitzit* helps us resist the ploys of the Adversary, and instead, pursue opportunities to share and grow. Instead of forgetting about the meaning of life, we begin to forget about the futile desires of the ego.

The four sets of fringes on the *Talit* and *Tzitzit* generate their power by acting as channels for the four letters that compose the Holiest Name of God, known as the Tetragrammaton.

Tefillin

Humankind is a microcosm of Creation. A person's right arm corresponds to the Right Column (+), the left arm embodies the Left Column (-), and the brain, the seat of human consciousness, corresponds to the Third and Central Column, known as resistance or free will. All forms of receiving and taking are channeled through the left side of the human body, and all forms of giving and sharing are rooted in the right side. Free will, where we resist selfish receiving (Left Column) and share instead (Right Column), is rooted in the realm of human consciousness (Central Column).

True consciousness occurs when we *resist*. If we merely take, which is our instinctive nature, we are behaving reactively. Consciousness elevates when we resist taking, and we think of others and share instead. That is the key to evolving and transforming the world.

However, because of the human ego—the force called Satan— we are not aware of the dangers of selfish receiving. The ego gives us pleasure and reward each time we receive at the expense of another, but when we receive we only acquire a limited, temporary form of pleasure. Conversely, when we share we experience a limited and temporary form of pain in the ego; afterwards, however, the Light of the Creator fills our life, bringing us genuine happiness in a practical, tangible way.

Unfortunately, our ego keeps us from seeing the payoff that accompanies resisting and sharing. The Adversary within focuses our attention and desires on the immediate moment, so that we sacrifice long-term happiness for short-term gratification.

Because the Left Column (the ego) is so powerful, we require additional tools to bind and control it. This is the purpose of *Tefillin*. Every morning, a man wraps the leather straps of the *Tefillin* around the left arm and hand in order to bind the negative Left-Column Desire that governs our nature. Combined with the various Names of God that are implanted within the *Tefillin* boxes and other prayer-connections performed at this time, the donning of the *Tefillin* is a powerful way to tame and transform the negative urges, self-centered desires, fears, anger, rage and mean-spiritedness that lurk deep within the various levels of the ego.

To help us understand with greater depth the power and purpose of *Tefillin*, let's examine one of the most controversial passages of the Bible.

Sacrifice

"Show me you love me. Show me you care. Go into your kitchen. Pull out a butcher knife. Slit your son's throat."

No, this is not the sequel to the movie *Scream 3*! This paraphrases what God, our Creator, asked the great patriarch Abraham to do to his beloved son Isaac. God told Abraham to sacrifice Isaac as a demonstration of Abraham's unwavering commitment to the Master of the Universe.

What happened to God's Commandment, "You shall not kill?" How do we—logical, rational, thinking people—reconcile God's order to Abraham with God's Commandment not to kill?

We don't reconcile it. We cannot make any sense out of this contradiction—at least not on the surface. Without Kabbalah's insights, there can be no practical benefit to readers of this biblical passage—which might explain why 95 percent of the world doesn't read it anymore. But the *Zohar* revealed a profound message, a secret that will help you to achieve a deep understanding of your own nature and find the keys to true happiness and sanity in this unhappy, insane world. This message will also shed some light on the purpose of *Tefillin* and the ways of the kabbalist.

In the traditional biblical story, Abraham follows God's order; he takes Isaac to Mount Moriah and binds him to an altar. Just as Abraham is about to lower the knife to the throat of his son, an angel arrives on the scene with an urgent message: "Stop! This was just a test from God." It was a very close call. But why would an all-loving, all-merciful God put a man through such an agonizing test just to demonstrate his loyalty, love and allegiance?

As we have seen throughout this book, the world according to Kabbalah is composed of three primary forces: a positive force, a negative force, and a neutral force. Science concurs with this view. These three forces express themselves both spiritually and physically. Physically, the three forces are expressed as the proton, the electron, and the neutron. Spiritually, the three forces are expressed as:

1. the desire to share (good);
2. the desire to receive (evil);
3. the free will to choose between the two (transformation).

These three forces are what distinguish humans from animals. A lion in hot pursuit of an antelope will not suddenly stop in its tracks to consider the moral implications of slaughtering the poor creature. Dinner is dinner. A human, however, often pauses to consider his or her actions. This stopping, or *resisting*, can only come about as a result of free will, which is an exclusive feature of the human race.

Kabbalah says that these three spiritual forces are the key to the secret meaning behind the biblical stories about Abraham, his son Isaac, and Isaac's son, Jacob. Abraham, Isaac and Jacob are the three great biblical patriarchs. But they are more than just names or characters in the Bible; they are also the template for these three principles. They are the wellspring from which these three forces emerge into human consciousness and this world. The scheme is as follows:

- Abraham signifies the Right Column force of sharing.
- Isaac signifies the Left Column force of receiving.
- Jacob signifies the Central Column force of balance.

In talking about Abraham, Isaac and Jacob, the Bible is actually talking about the human being. It is talking about you and me. Let's now reexamine the story of Isaac and the sacrifice to unlock the secrets within it. *The code*: God commanded Abraham to bind Isaac upon the altar and kill him as a sacrifice. *The true inner meaning*: A human must constantly use the power of the soul (Abraham) to bind his or her desire (the binding of Isaac) and eliminate all selfish, self-destructive traits from his or her nature (the slaughtering of Isaac). This entails giving up (sacrificing) short-term pleasures in return for eternal spiritual pleasures. Does that mean no more cars, stereos, houses, clothes, cell phones or home computers? Of course not. Just as Abraham did not have to actually go through with the sacrifice of his son, we do not have to give up the entire physical world. It's the *addiction* to that world, our all-consuming self-interest, which has to be slaughtered.

We love our own ego the way one loves a beloved son—the way Abraham loved Isaac. Once we sacrifice the ego, once this addictive aspect of our nature is gone, the angel comes and says, *Okay, keep the car. Keep the house. Keep the clothes. Keep the plasma TV and the iPhone.* It's okay for us to keep these material items now, because they do not control our degree of happiness. When we appreciate true spiritual freedom and pleasure, then we can have it all. The only thing to give up in the physical world is the ego, which keeps us addicted to external items so that they control us, instead of the kabbalist's way around.

On the path of Kabbalah, our happiness is created from within. We are the captains of our fate and the creators of our fulfillment. The more negative traits that we "sacrifice" within ourselves, the more we will be able to receive the lasting Light of fulfillment.

How to Have It All

A kabbalist wants it all. That is what the way of the kabbalist is designed to achieve. Kabbalah never asks us to trade down in life. When we give up our ego, we might initially feel that we are giving up something of value, but we're not. All we're doing is exchanging hamburger for steak. We are being given something that will make us far happier than our wildest dreams.

Each time we indulge our ego we trade away a true spiritual treasure—health, happy kids, inner peace of mind, freedom from anxiety, and true prosperity, for starters. On the other hand, each time we resist and deny our ego, we receive a priceless spiritual treasure in return. However, grasping this profound truth and living by it is easier said than done. The ego is strong, and the pleasures that gratify it are powerfully tempting and quite seductive.

When we wrap the leather straps of *Tefillin* on our left arm, we bind and triumph over all the negative emotions, desires, fears and anxieties that rule this life. We are imitating the binding of Isaac: our right arm (Abraham) is binding *Tefillin* around our left arm (Isaac) for the sole purpose of slaughtering all the negative traits that lead us to darkness, personal destruction, and eventual death. Once we remove all aspects of negative desire—once our Right Column energy rules, controls, and directs the Left Column—we will have achieved immortality.

Demand nothing less.

part three
work week

The Sabbath (*Shabbat*)

According to Kabbalah, the Sabbath serves one purpose: to remove chaos, pain and death from the landscape of human existence. The Sabbath is not a day of rest, but rather a day of intense spiritual labor. The only thing that we truly seek to bring to its final rest is death itself. The Sabbath was given to humankind to help us achieve that lofty aim.

If you plant an apple seed in the ground, an apple tree inevitably appears. However, once the roots, trunk and branches emerge, you can no longer find the original seed of the tree. It has disappeared. The *Cause* of the tree has vanished from our sight. Kabbalah, however, says you can find the original Cause by looking at the final Effect. What is the final Effect of an apple seed? It is the apple dangling at the end of a branch. And sure enough, if you look inside the apple, what do you find? You find the original *Cause* of the tree—an apple seed! This phenomenon illustrates the Law of Cause and Effect: the Cause contains the Effect (the tiny seed contains the entire tree inside it), and the Effect contains the Cause (the final apple contains the seed).

Thirty four hundred years ago at Mount Sinai, Moses and the Tablets created a state of immortality and unimaginable happiness. As mentioned previously, the *Zohar* says these Tablets, which were made of gleaming sapphire, transmitted the metaphysical energy of the 99 Percent Reality into our physical reality. This energy transmission produced a perfect state of immortality. Death was banished from the landscape of human civilization.

However, after the Israelites built the golden calf, Moses dropped the two Tablets, and they shattered. As a result humankind was disconnected from the Light of immortality; death was reborn. The *Zohar* and the kabbalists of antiquity tell us that Moses put the shattered pieces of the Tablets into the Ark of the Covenant before going back up the mountain and receiving a second set of Tablets from God. Both the original broken Tablets and the Second Tablets contained the Light of Immortality. Both sets were then put inside the Ark of the Covenant, and the Ark was buried in the ground, like a seed. From this seed emerged the branches and fruits that are Torah scrolls.

The Light of Immortality was the *Cause* of the Tablets and the Ark. The final Effect, or fruit, of this Cause is the Torah scroll that is read on the Sabbath. When you look inside an apple, you find the original Cause of the apple—an apple seed. When you look inside the Torah, you find the original Cause of the Torah—*the force of immortality!*

This is why we read the Torah every Sabbath. It restores a portion of the Light of immortality that was lost on Mount Sinai as a result of the building of the golden calf. The golden calf is a code for the human ego. We worship the ego and its self-serving desires the way the Israelites worshipped the golden calf. Thus, each Sabbath—that is, every seventh day (which corresponds to the seventh dimension, *Malchut*)—we partake of the Light of Immortality in order to cleanse a portion of ego that causes us to worship the material world and the ego itself. As the ego is washed away, the Light of Immortality is increased in the world. When we achieve a critical mass of people who are properly using the technology of the Torah and the Sabbath, death will be banished from this world.

It is only your ego, Satan, which makes you doubt this truth. Cynicism, skepticism, and doubt are manufactured by our Adversary—the same doubt the ancient Israelites had regarding Moses—for this is one of Satan's favorite weapons. As we overcome our skepticism, the achievability of immortality and unending happiness become tangible in our minds. Every single week, the Torah and the Sabbath connection banish a portion of our doubts.

The Sabbath Structure

Like everything else in the *Way of the Kabbalist*, the Sabbath is founded upon the Three Column System which serves to generate Light. Friday night prayer connections and meal establish the Left Column energy of receiving, which is completed by the drinking and blessing of a cup of red wine. The blessing said over the wine contains exactly seventy-two words, and each word connects to one of the 72 Names of God. This blessing channels the Light of the 99 Percent into our reality because red wine has the innate capacity to attract spiritual energy through its receiving power, which is one reason it can make us drunk.

The Right Column is constructed during the Saturday morning Torah reading and meal. The Third Meal, during the late afternoon on the Sabbath, creates the third and Central Column, the filament, which makes possible the illumination of the Light of the Sabbath.

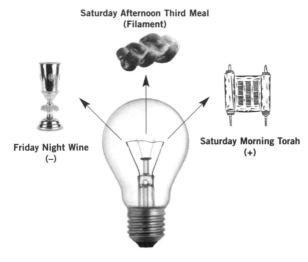

Saturday Afternoon Third Meal
(Filament)

Friday Night Wine
(−)

Saturday Morning Torah
(+)

BUILDING A SPIRITUAL LIGHT BULB

For details on the Sabbath, see the book *Kabbalah on the Sabbath*.

Baking the Sabbath Bread (*Challah*)

Prior to the Sabbath, women bake egg-based bread called *Challah*. This action helps women correct the original sin of Eve, which was tasting the fruit of the *Tree of Knowledge*. Kabbalists tell us that this tree contained wheat. Therefore, by turning wheat into *Challah* for the Sabbath, Eve's sin is being corrected, as wheat becomes a conduit for channeling the Light of the Creator. Furthermore, *Challah*, like any bread, is a powerful antenna for drawing energy, so *Challah* is used to draw the Light and energy of the Sabbath into this physical reality. The only way to draw the Light into our physical reality is to create a conduit between our reality and the spiritual world. *Challah* is the conduit that allows us to harness Divine Energy and express it as spiritual Light.

Weekday Torah Readings

During the Sabbath, we capture enough Light and energy to last us an entire week. This is akin to charging a battery so that it lasts a long time. However, to use a battery you must establish the proper connections. To tap into our Divine battery that was charged up during the Sabbath, we read the Torah on Mondays and Thursdays during our morning prayer-connections so that we can use this power in a practical way all week long.

The second purpose behind the two weekly Torah readings is to establish an unbroken link from one Sabbath to the next. As mentioned earlier, death is also defined as space, so we do not want to create a space between one Sabbath and the next. Thus, we do not allow three full days (corresponding to the Three Column System) to transpire without some connection to the Torah. Otherwise, the Three Column System works against us by creating a complete structure of *space* that disconnects us from the source of all Light.

part four

monthly
cycle

The Head of the Month (*Rosh Chodesh*)

If you plant a defective apple seed, you can be sure that a defective apple tree will be the result, since the quality of the seed determines the quality and health of the tree.

Each new beginning, including each new month, is another new tree, and all the events in our lives that transpire throughout the month can be likened to the branches. The results of the work that we do are the fruits of the trees. We all want to ensure that the fruits of our labor are bountiful and of the highest quality in terms of happiness, fulfillment and success. Therefore, our entire month depends on the quality of the seeds we plant.

Kabbalists revealed that each month contains an actual seed. That seed is the first day of the month, known as the Head of the Month (*Rosh Chodesh*). If we take control of the head of the month and plant a quality seed, we wind up controlling the next twenty-nine or so days so that we'll have a high-quality, spiritually successful month.

The twelve months of the year correspond directly to the twelve signs of the Zodiac. Each Zodiac sign contains both positive and negative influences. The *Rosh Chodesh* connection gives us the ability to tap into the positive influences of the month so as to resist, overcome and transform negative influences. We make this connection and achieve this power by accessing the very building blocks of creation.

The Building Blocks

Earlier we learned that just as various combinations of matter and energy make up the entire world, the Hebrew letters in their various configurations form the very building blocks of the spiritual and material universe. Each letter is an expression of a particular cosmic force, imbued with intelligence and consciousness that both creates and sustains the cosmos. Through conscious meditation upon the Hebrew letters, we attain control over the metaphysical forces prevalent during different months of the year. Some four thousand years ago, Abraham the Patriarch revealed in *Sefer Yetzirah* (*Book of Formation*) the DNA-like combinations of letters that create and control the astrological influences of the twelve months and the twelve signs of the Zodiac. Simple meditation upon the two-letter DNA codes for each month, combined with a special monthly Torah reading, gives us the power to control the month and all of its influences.

See below for the letters that govern each month.

Scorpio	Aries	Pisces	Sagittarius	Aquarius	Capricorn
Mar-Hesvan	Nisan	Adar	Kislev	Shevat	Tevet
דנ	הה	קג	סג	צב	עב

Cancer	Virgo	Gemini	Libra	Taurus	Leo
Tammuz	Elul	Sivan	Tishrey	Iyar	Av
חות	רי	רו	פל	פו	כט

← Scanning Direction

Blessing of the New Moon

The Earth is governed by the moon's monthly cycle. Each month, kabbalists bless the moon usually seven days after *Rosh Chodesh*. By actively blessing the moon in Hebrew, we seize control over it. The moon has no light of its own, only that which it receives from the sun. We are like the moon in that we receive all of our Light from the Creator. The Blessing of the Moon allows us to rise above all negative influences that emanate from this lunar body. In addition, it hastens the arrival of world peace and immortality by injecting the moon (and all humankind) with the ability to transform the *Desire to Receive* (signified by the moon) into the *Desire to Receive for the Sake of Sharing*.

part five

the yearly
cycle

Rosh Hashanah and Yom Kippur, Succoth, Simchat Torah—the whole period of the holidays is actually one process of building our spiritual Vessel to receive total fulfillment in the coming year. It uses all of the spiritual foundation to enable us to remove the negativity and create a Vessel to be filled with Light.

Rosh Hashanah, traditionally known as the "Jewish New Year," is also understood as a time of judgment when the Creator supposedly makes a reckoning of our deeds during the previous year. But according to Kabbalah, both of these depictions of Rosh Hashanah are grossly inaccurate.

The Force we call God does not preside over a heavenly court that decides who will be forgiven and who will be punished. Furthermore, Rosh Hashanah actually occurs in the seventh month of the Hebrew calendar; so it does not signify a new year. Nor does Rosh Hashanah have anything to do with a specific religious faith, such as Judaism.

What then are we to make of the commonly held notions that Rosh Hashanah is a "new year" and a time of "judgment?"

The Court of Cause and Effect Is Now in Session

Science can offer us some insight into the true significance of Rosh Hashanah. A basic principle of physics, Newton's Third Law, states that for every action there is an equal and opposite reaction; for every Cause there is an Effect. Rosh Hashanah is built upon this Universal Law as well.

When we behave in a contemptuous, uncivil or rude manner we arouse negative forces even though we may not be aware of it. When we cheat, lie, steal or harm other people, a negative energy comes into existence. Each time we lose our patience, react with anger or lose our temper we create an actual force of darkness that clings to us. These negative forces are the unseen cause of all the things that just happen to go wrong in our lives.

Rosh Hashanah is our opportunity to go back and dig up those negative seeds we have planted before they reach fruition. On this day, we can eradicate all the negative energy and blockages caused by the selfish acts we've committed during the preceding year. At this special time, the universe is structured so that the consequences of our careless misdeeds, intolerant behavior, and hurtful words return to us to be addressed. We also have the ability to plant a new seed for the coming year.

The fact is that on *Rosh Hashanah* the repercussions of our own actions are presented for judgment by *us*—not judgment by the Creator!

Rather than finding ourselves sitting in the docket of a heavenly court, we find ourselves sitting as judges in the court of Cause and Effect. Every action we perform is a boomerang we fling out into the universe. Each *Rosh Hashanah*, all of these many boomerangs return to our lives—all the positive ones and all the negative ones. Moreover, this experience of *Rosh Hashanah* is not exclusive to any one religion. According to the kabbalistic sages, all humankind shares a heightened experience of Cause and Effect during this time.

Kabbalah teaches that reality is a mirror. Look into a mirror and smile and the image smiles back. If we curse into the mirror, the image curses back. God never inflicts punishment upon us or stands in judgment of us. It is our own negative actions that rebound into our lives as reflections bouncing back from the cosmic mirror. When we perform a negative act in our world, the cosmic mirror reflects that negative energy back at us during *Rosh Hashanah*.

This is why the connection known as *Rosh Hashanah* occurs during the astrological sign of Libra. Libra is represented by the scales, which are taking the weight of positive energy versus negative energy, both of which are generated by our actions. We, not the Creator, control which way the scales tip.

Crime and Punishment

God does not punish. We can never repeat this truth enough. Neither does God reward. According to Kabbalah, there is only one Force, one Divine Energy Source for the entire cosmos. This Force is only good, positive and infinitely compassionate. Most people call this infinite force "God."

Consider this. Electricity enriches your life by providing power for all your home appliances. But this same force can also be destructive and harmful if you stick your finger into a light socket. If you did, it would be senseless to say that the electricity punished you. The nature of the electricity never changed. In the same way, the Creator never punishes us. We ourselves have chosen, knowingly or unknowingly through our selfish actions, to place our finger in the electrical socket.

We always have free choice when it comes to how we react (or proact) to life's challenges.

Did you ever notice that even when we know something is wrong, we often choose to do it anyway? Whether it's losing our temper, overeating, oversleeping, overworking, or overreacting to a petty slight or setback, sometimes we obey our selfish urges even though we know we shouldn't. Similarly, even when we know something is right, correct, good, or beneficial to us, we sometimes forsake it for the negative option? Or we put it off until we forget about it completely? We procrastinate. Delay. Postpone. And dally.

We always have the freedom of choice to engage in either negative actions or positive actions. But there is a dark, dangerous force that constantly attempts to persuade us to act negatively.

Let's now define the whole concept of negative activity, which will show us how we inadvertently perform misdeeds each day of our lives.

Crimes and Misdemeanors

Negative activity can manifest in ways both large and small. For instance, consider murder, evil speech and adultery. These are some of the "sins" we are supposedly atoning for on *Rosh Hashanah*. The kabbalist, however, has a different perspective.

Let's first examine *murder*. We can kill someone physically, or we can kill someone emotionally and spiritually. We can assassinate a person, or we can assassinate a person's character—

and who doesn't enjoy gossiping about other people? We can destroy someone's relationships through gossip, or we can ruin their livelihood when we cheat them in business.

Kabbalah teaches that the sin of "spilling blood" is not limited to physical violence. "Spilling blood" also refers to the shame and embarrassment we cause to others, forcing the blood to rush to their faces out of humiliation when we snap at them or demean when we act out our own insecurities and selfishness.

According to Kabbalah, any form of nasty speech or gossip—even about someone we have never met—is one of the most serious crimes a person can commit. Speech has tremendous powers. When we speak badly of others, we not only damage their lives; we also damage ourselves and the rest of the world. At *Rosh Hashanah*, these damaging words come back to haunt us. You can deny this if you wish, but disbelief in the law of gravity will not prevent you from crashing into the pavement if you step off a skyscraper. Evil speech is a no-win situation, and each time we engage in it, we pay for it. As a wise saying tells us, *"People should be more concerned with what comes out of their mouths than what goes into their mouths."*

Let's now examine the sin of envy. Envy is not limited to coveting someone else's spouse. One can also covet another person's business, children or material possessions. Envy and adultery occur when we fail fully to appreciate all that we have. This lack of appreciation takes place when we view our possessions through an egocentric lens, when we believe that these are a reflection of who we really are. When you feel this way and you cast your eye on the possessions of another, you covet them because you believe that if you could have them you would be more than you are now. Kabbalah teaches us that coveting the spouse of another person or another partner if you are married, is a form of adultery.

Copping a Plea

Now that we understand that there are real repercussions associated with our negative actions, large and small, we may be tempted to ask for a pardon due to our former ignorance of the Law of Cause and Effect. Unfortunately, ignorance of the law is no excuse. The natural laws of the universe cannot be violated without consequences. It does you no good to plead ignorance of the law of electricity while you are touching a live high-voltage wire.

However, it is also a spiritual law of the universe that when a person achieves a basic change in his or her own nature the universe must respond and reflect that transformative energy back to us. We can then use that energy to alter our destiny and deflect judgments.

The first thing we must do to bring about change is to admit that we're blameworthy.

We need to accept responsibility.

We have to become accountable for our actions—especially the ones we are not even aware of! That is perhaps the hardest thing to do.

And especially during the *Rosh Hashanah* connection we must find as many negative traits as possible dwelling within ourselves, and make every attempt with our heart and soul to change our ways.

This internal change begins with a majestic blast of a horn.

The Secret of the *Shofar*

Most people view the blowing of the *Shofar* as a ceremonial tradition, a symbolic act of commemoration. Nothing could be further from the truth. Because we have remained ignorant of the true purpose of the *Shofar*, its effect in our lives has been negligible. Two thousand years of pain and suffering are evidence of that harsh truth. Instead of being an awesome instrument of power, the *Shofar* has remained a fruitless symbol of an impotent tradition.

The *Shofar*'s power can only be expressed when knowledge of its true purpose is instilled within our consciousness. Knowing why we sound the *Shofar* is the electrical current that turns it on. Knowledge powers the *Shofar*!

In essence, the *Shofar* is a weapon right out of Star Wars—not the movie, but like the U.S. military's Strategic Defense Initiative of the 1980s. The military envisioned satellites orbiting the planet that could use lasers to shoot down missiles launched at the United States. In spiritual terms, these missiles correspond to judgment headed our way; more specifically, their targets are the negative blockages embedded in our soul as a result of our egocentric behavior throughout the previous year.

Unlike laser satellites that shoot down missiles, the *Shofar* goes one better and removes the targets themselves! In other words, the *Shofar* banishes all those blockages from our inner being. The sound emanating from the *Shofar* operates like a spiritual laser beam that dissolves all the negative energy we've created over the previous twelve months—provided that we own up to all of our internal garbage and take responsibility for it.

The mystical sound of the *Shofar* acts as a cleansing agent, a mystical sonic vibration that permeates every crack and crevice in our being, removing negative residues and purifying our soul. Once these blockages are removed, the judgments have lost their targets and the missiles coming our way have nowhere to go!

This is precisely what the sound of the *Shofar* accomplishes in the Upper Worlds. However, there are two prerequisites that must be met before the *Shofar* can perform its true function.

1. A genuine desire to change our ways is one of the forces that activates the power of the *Shofar*. If we don't really want to change, the sound is useless and we will receive no benefit.

2. If we don't have complete certainty of the *Shofar*'s power our doubts become a self-fulfilling prophecy, and *Rosh Hashanah* remains the same old tradition that it has been for thousands of years—a boring, uninspiring, irrelevant tradition that has somehow survived into the modern world.

It's Not about a New Year

According to Kabbalah, the month of *Nissan* (Aries) until *Tishrei* (Libra) is the male aspect of the year, or the time when we plant seeds. The second half of the year, the time following *Rosh Hashanah*, is the female aspect of the year, when the effects of our seeds are manifested. *Rosh Hashanah* is a gift that allows us to use the technology of the *Shofar* to go back to the creation of the world—before the negativity we planted lifetime after lifetime—to a time of our own perfection. This way, if we have sincerely transformed in these two days using the technology made available to us by the kabbalists, we can enter the second half of the year cleansed. A huge opportunity, this reveals the true mercy of the Creator and the spiritual system provided for us to achieve total fulfillment by our own hand.

Contrary to popular belief, *Rosh Hashanah* is not the "new year." *Rosh* means "head," indicating that *Rosh Hashanah* is the head or seed of the year. The seed you plant on *Rosh Hashanah* grows into the tree that will be the coming year. As an apple seed begets an apple tree, a negative seed begets a negative year, and a positive seed generates a positive year. *Rosh Hashanah* is our opportunity to choose the seed we wish to plant. The harder we work at changing our ways and removing our negative traits, the more positive energy we inject into the seed. Then the seed sprouts, and our year blossoms with peace and prosperity instead of chaos and strife.

For this reason, *Rosh Hashanah* occurs on the first day of the Hebrew month *Tishrei*. Although this month is the seventh month of the year in the Hebrew calendar, *Tishrei* is known as the "head" of all months. The *Shofar* helps illustrate this connection. The *Shofar* is actually a ram's horn, taken from the *head* of a ram. Why a ram? The ram is the symbol of the Zodiac sign of Aries, which corresponds to the Hebrew month of *Nissan*; and *Nissan* represents the true New Year in the Hebrew calendar. So, in a way, we do connect to the concept of a new year on *Rosh Hashanah*, but we do so on a seed level.

Let's recap what we've learned about *Rosh Hashanah*:

- Over these two days we have access to the power of the *new year*, signified by the ram's horn, which connects us to astrological sign of Aries and the Hebrew month of *Nissan*, the true new year.

- We also have access to the power associated with the *head of the year*, signified by the Hebrew month of *Tishrei*, and the fact the *Shofar* comes from the *head* of the ram.

A few dozen blasts of the *Shofar*, coupled with our sincere effort to transform our negative traits, give us unparalleled power to influence our lives. On *Rosh Hashanah,* we control the seed, the head, of the entire year to come. And we rise above the influences of the stars and planets.

World Peace

According to the *Zohar*, the entire planet is a mirror of the human body, and Israel is the counterpart of the human heart. Just as the heart supplies purified blood to nourish the body,

Israel furnishes spiritual Light to aid, nourish and heal all the nations of the world. If Israel does not furnish spiritual Light to the nations, they rise up against her, just as the body responds with disease if toxic blood courses through our veins. This is why the Land of Israel, although tiny relative to the rest of the world, has been the center of world attention for thousands of years.

As we learned earlier, sincere effort to transform our negativity can remove blockages from our arteries. On *Rosh Hashanah*, our sincere effort to transform combines with the sounds of the *Shofar* to remove barriers between Israel and all nations of the world, clearing the way for lasting peace in the Middle East and for global harmony.

In other words, peace does not begin with fund-raising dinners, politics, wars, intellectual debate or organizations that have appointed themselves to represent the people. Peace begins with the man in the mirror! Personal peace is the only effective cause of world peace. Personal peace and personal health lead to global peace and global health. Everything is interconnected.

Another Ancient Secret of the *Shofar*

According to the *Zohar*, the human body is a mirror of the Ten *Sefirot*, the ten dimensions that constitute all reality. Each body part corresponds to another dimension or spiritual world. The *Zohar* says the esophagus corresponds to the dimension that is our physical world, known as *Malchut*. Why? Because the physical materials of food and liquid travel down the esophagus whenever we eat and drink.

The *Zohar* also says the *trachea* corresponds to the dimension known as *Binah*, the 99 Percent Reality, a spiritual dimension so filled with Light, joy and Divine Energy that there is absolutely no need for nourishment there. Remember, the trachea is merely a windpipe; no food or drink travel through it. Similarly there is no need for food or drink in *Binah*, where the Light itself provides more pleasure and nourishment than the human mind can conceive.

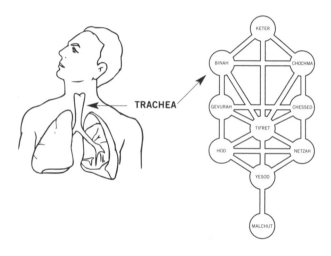

The Hebrew word for esophagus, *Veshet*, is spelled with the letters *Vav*, *Shin*, and *Tet*.

The *Zohar* explains that when we are overly self-indulgent, allowing our ego and selfish desires to grow, the letter *Vav* mirrors this malignant growth by extending its length, so that it becomes the letter *Nun*.

Veshet (Esophagus)

VAV grows to a NUN

When *Vav* is turned into a *Nun*, the letters that spell esophagus (*Veshet*) are now rearranged to spell *Satan* (*Sin, Tet, Nun*).

(SATAN)

As our ego grows, as our reactive nature grows, as our mood swings grow, so too does the letter *Vav* grow in the word esophagus. The *Zohar* states that when our physical desires run rampant and we choose the physical world over the spiritual, the negative force known as Satan (also known as *space* or *chaos*) grows so large that it overcomes "all the limbs and the arteries" for all the 365 days of the solar year. "Esophagus" (*Veshet*) metamorphoses into "Satan," creating chaos in our health, space between the atoms in our body, strife in our careers, trouble in our marriages, and plain old darkness.

But there is recourse for the remorseful heart: the *Shofar*. Like the trachea, the *Shofar* is a windpipe. The only thing that enters both of them is air. In the same way that the trachea is the connection to *Binah*, the blowing of the *Shofar* also connects us to *Binah*, the 99 Percent Reality of the Light. Through the power of the *Shofar* on *Rosh Hashanah* the letter *Nun* in the word *Satan* is reduced in size—just as we reduce our ego during *Rosh Hashanah*—and it reverts back into a *Vav*, again permitting the word to spell *esophagus* in Hebrew. Satan, space, and the force of death are thereby extracted from our arteries.

Notice the uncanny similarities between the letter *Vav*, the *Shofar*, and the human trachea:

VAV   **SHOFAR**   **TRACHEA**

Yom Kippur

Yom Kippur is not a day of fasting, mourning or atoning. Rather, it is a day of *feasting*. We feast on five gigantic meals during this powerful day of connection. However, the meals that we consume are of a spiritual nature. We receive our spiritual nourishment from the highest levels of the spiritual atmosphere, from the realm of *Binah*. This nourishment gives us the sustenance we need for the manifestation of our fulfillment, health, wealth, and family for the next twelve months.

To allow our soul to reach the spiritual heights known as *Binah*, we must literally ground our body's awareness so that the soul can break free and rise to the highest of heights, where it achieves oneness with *Binah*. This is the real meaning behind the word "atonement." Atonement literally means *at-onement*, or *oneness*.

On *Yom Kippur*, from sundown to sundown, we have a window of time to grasp all this light. We do not eat, drink, engage in sex, wash, or wear perfumes, lotions, or leather shoes. We reduce the influence of the body as much as possible so that our true self—our consciousness and soul—can successfully reach *Binah* and dine on the five hearty meals of Light. These five meals are transferred to us by virtue of the various Hebrew and Aramaic prayer-connections and the Torah readings that take place during *Yom Kippur*.

The other vital aspect of *Yom Kippur* is the canceling of the vows, also known as the *Kol Nedrei*. In traditional circles, people come to hear this "prayer" that is said in Aramaic without understanding that this connection obliterates all the spaces we created within ourselves by the commitments we did not keep. Each time we make a promise, we create a Vessel. If we follow through, we fill that Vessel with Light, but when we do not follow through, the Vessel remains empty. Empty spaces are filled with darkness, so the more promises we fail to keep, the more darkness exists within us. Most of the chaos in our lives is a result of spaces created by our unfulfilled vows. For instance, promising to take out the garbage and then failing to do it is an instance of an unfulfilled vow.

On *Yom Kippur*, all the empty vessels created by broken promises, unfulfilled commitments and empty vows are hanging over our head. In order to ensure that the next twelve months of our lives contain no empty space or darkness, *Yom Kippur* undoes the effects of all these broken vows, filling up the empty spaces with energy so that darkness and the force called Satan cannot enter. We, in effect, elevate to the state of *Binah* and become completely pure. The Rav said once that on Yom Kippur the whole world becomes pure, not just those observing the holiday. Such is the energy of that day. There is no Satan on *Yom Kippur*, because the whole world is elevated to the *Sefira* of *Binah*, as if in a *mikveh*—immersed in Light. But as with immersing in a physical *mikveh*, if we don't have an awareness of what is required from us to tap into this awesome Light, and if we still behave in our robotic way driven by memory impulses—even though Satan is not present—we lose all the Light that we just bathed in.

Connection with the Chickens (*Kapparot*)

In the middle of the night, the day before *Yom Kippur*, a kabbalist takes a chicken and performs what is known as *Kapparot*, holding the chicken up and rotating it counterclockwise over his head while reciting a blessing. This transfers the energy of the kabbalist to the chicken. All the negative actions performed over the previous year are now infused in the chicken. After the ritual is complete, the chicken is slaughtered and given to charity as food for the poor. Parents with children under the age of thirteen perform this action on behalf of the children.

For the chicken, this is considered a "holy" action that elevates the spark of Light in the chicken to its next level.

Succoth

This seven-day holiday follows *Yom Kippur.* Each of the seven days connects to one of the seven dimensions (*Sefirot*) that directly influence our reality. During the connection of *Succoth* we receive what kabbalists call Surrounding Light and Inner Light for the entire year to come. Surrounding Light helps us from the outside to expand our spiritual capacity to hold more Light and achieve our fullest spiritual potential for the coming year. Inner Light protects our innate Light from inside, while also pushing us to expand our Vessel so that we can hold more Surrounding Light.

During the seven days of *Succoth,* it is as if a spiritual bank vault containing Surrounding Light and Inner Light has been opened, and we are free to take as much of that energy as possible. This is achieved by spending as much time as possible, and making as many spiritual connections as possible, in a *Sukkah*, a temporary structure built according to specific requirements so that it can act as a spiritual power generator. Simply by sitting, sleeping and eating in the *Sukkah*, the body and soul are nourished with enough Surrounding and Inner Light to last for the entire year to come. In terms of power and energy, sitting inside the *Sukkah* is just like sitting inside the original Temple of Jerusalem, which was the energy generator for the entire world.

Rejoicing with the Torah (*Simchat Torah*)

Now that we have planted our seed for the entire year at *Rosh Hashanah*, cancelled all of our vows and eaten five meals that will give us energy for the next year at *Yom Kippur*, and secured as much Surrounding Light and Inner Light as possible for the next twelve months at *Succoth*, the last goal is to capture as much joy and happiness as we can for the year ahead. This is the purpose of the connection known as *Simchat Torah*.

This connection occurs on the last day of *Succoth*, when men and women literally dance with the Torah with as much joy and happiness as they can. They do this because the amount of joy we express during this time is the amount of joy we draw to ourselves. The more joy we express, the more we fill up our Happy Bank Account for the year to come. During *Simchat Torah* there is a Torah reading and various prayer-connections, but the main feature is a party atmosphere where singing and dancing with the Torah become the ultimate technology for securing a year's worth of happiness.

Chanukah

From the kabbalistic point of view, *Chanukah* is the time of year when the spiritual energy of *miracle* is released into the universe. This miracle energy can be harnessed to produce miracles in our own lives. *Chanukah* has nothing to do with commemorating a miracle in history, or any other tradition. *Chanukah* is technology, plain and simple. By lighting candles and implementing a few other kabbalistic practices, we connect our souls to the miracle energy prevalent in the cosmos for the eight days of this profound event. The kabbalists also tell us that *Chanukah* is a mini–*Rosh Hashanah*, allowing us to redeem any spiritual debts we might have overlooked during *Rosh Hashanah*. Thankfully, the universe has been constructed so that we are constantly given chances to correct all the misdeeds we have committed, knowingly or unknowingly.

The New Year for the Trees (*Tu BiShevat*)

Kabbalistically speaking, trees are so important to this Earth that the Bible designated a calendar just for the trees. The new year of the trees is an actual holiday, or, as we understand it kabbalistically, a day of connection. This holiday occurs on the fifteenth day of the Hebrew month of Aquarius (*Shevat*), the day when trees and our environment receive their spiritual nourishment for the entire year. This is the time where we take care of our environment spiritually.

For humankind this day is an opportunity to connect to the consciousness of the trees. We can benefit from this connection because trees embody a consciousness, intelligence and energy that allow them to rise to great heights, despite even the pull of gravity. Gravity, according to Kabbalah, is a force that makes us *take* without sharing; gravity is a Left Column force of pure receiving. Planting a tree and eating the fruit of a tree on the day of the *New Year of the Trees* instills within us the power and strength to resist and rise up against our own gravitational pull—the ego—the limited consciousness that only sees oneself and not the whole. So not only do the trees help us on an environmental level, but on the day of their New Year, when we eat their fruits and nuts, they also share with us their unique consciousness.

Purim

Purim actually comes from the word *Yom Kippurim*, which is the proper name for *Yom Kippur*. In English, *Yom Kippurim* basically means "almost like *Purim*." Most people mistakenly believe that *Yom Kippur* is the highest or holiest day of the year, but this is not quite true. The very name of the event tells us that it is *almost* like *Purim*. A stunning secret emerges from this definition: *Purim* is a higher connection to the Light of the 99 Percent Reality.

Purim embodies the essence of the time of the Messiah—heaven on Earth. During the connection of *Purim*, we read from the biblical scroll of Esther. Afterward, everyone gets drunk to the point that they are beyond intellectual judgments, to mimic the realm of true reality, where there is no need to discriminate because there is only good. When we drink to the point where we are beyond rational awareness, our consciousness rises above the realm of *knowledge* and reaches the spiritual dimension the kabbalists call *nothingness* or *endlessness*, where all of existence is one undifferentiated whole. In this realm, darkness and all negative traits revert to their undifferentiated state of goodness. *Purim* gives us the opportunity to experience this undifferentiated state and transform all of our reactive traits, fears, anxieties and anger into positive qualities of love, courage, inner peace and unconditional love for others. Kabbalists tell us that when the Messiah arrives, the only holiday that will remain is *Purim*.

During *Purim* everyone joins in a masquerade as part of the festivities. One of the reasons for the costume is quite profound, based on the concept of God and the force we call Satan. Consider, for a moment, that one has to believe in God in order to serve God. An atheist is not going to follow the instructions of God. However, one does not have to believe in the existence of Satan in order to serve Satan. In fact, the opposite is true: if we did believe in the existence of Satan, we would *never* serve him. Therefore, our lack of belief in Satan strengthens him.

The kabbalists tell us that Satan's primary essence is doubt. Doubt and skepticism radiate from his very presence. The closer we get to him, the greater our doubt becomes—especially concerning his existence. It's the ultimate defense mechanism, making his task that much easier. The only reason we hurt other people is because we do not know that it is Satan (ego) who is motivating our behavior and the behavior of the people who irritate us.

The kabbalists are clear about this: immortality and world peace will only be achieved when enough people recognize the hidden force of Satan in their lives. The truth is, we didn't come to this world to *defeat* Satan; merely *discovering* him is enough. Once we know that he is the sole cause of our problems, we'll automatically ask the Light of the Creator to banish him, and then he will be destroyed.

This is why overcoming doubt is both the most important and the most challenging work in life. When we are first told that Satan exists as a potent force in the universe and that Satan is really our ego, and that our ego is not part of our true selves but instead exists separately from us—we doubt these propositions—thus strengthening Satan and the ego. But the ego is indeed separate from us, much like a costume we wear. We can put the costume on or take it off whenever we want to, but only if we know that the costume is merely a costume and not an integral part of who we are.

This is one reason why we wear a costume on *Purim*. We are admitting the existence of ego, and displaying it symbolically as a costume, instead of protecting and hiding it. During a costume party, we all know that everyone there is not what they pretend to be. But in life, when someone annoys us, we don't recognize that it's the costume—that is, the ego, or Satan—that is motivating the individual. Rarely do we recognize the costumes worn by our enemies, our friends or ourselves.

This is why we take everything so personally in life. This is why we judge others so harshly. We don't see that it is Satan inciting our behavior as well as that of our enemy, so we continue arguing, fighting and pouring more darkness into the world. If we truly saw the hand of the Adversary influencing the actions of all combatants, we would help our enemies and love them unconditionally. This is why the most important weapon the Adversary has is our disbelief in his existence. As long as we don't recognize his presence and influence, he is given a free hand to create havoc in our affairs.

On *Purim* we are given a powerful insight into true reality. When we're drunk—happily dancing and partying—we feel tremendous love for everyone. The costumes tell us that this state of contented existence can be ours forever if we just start recognizing that we are so much more than we appear to be. The moment Satan is no longer hidden, the world is transformed, and the Messiah arrives.

This is the true message and power of *Purim*!

The Passover Connection

The traditional story of Passover tells of slavery, exile, and eventual freedom for the Israelites who fled the land of Egypt. Traditionally, this slavery has been depicted as brutally hard work performed under cruel overseers wielding slashing whips. The ancient kabbalists, however, brought to light some interesting facts that have largely been overlooked by rabbis, priests and scholars alike.

On the literal level, the Passover story tells us that the Israelites were in bondage in Egypt for four hundred years. They were captives of the hard-hearted pharaohs who ruled Egypt. Then God sent a great leader named Moses to free the Israelites. Moses led the Israelites out of Egypt and took them on a long, arduous journey, beginning with a famous sojourn across the bottom of the safely-parted Red Sea. The Israelites eventually arrived at Mount Sinai, where they had a date with destiny.

But here's the interesting part: the Israelites taste freedom for the first time in centuries, yet they begin whining and complaining the moment it gets a little hot and dry in the desert. They even beg Moses to take them back to Egypt! Are we to believe the Israelites actually had it pretty good in Egypt? Was life in the desert worse than slavery in Egypt?

Something isn't right. The literal story doesn't make sense. Yet, year after year, we're supposed to recount this dubious story at the holiday known as Passover.

The revered Kabbalist Rav Isaac Luria (also known as The Ari) saw the same discrepancies; he asked the same questions and discovered some very illuminating answers.

Unraveling the Code

The Ari revealed that the entire biblical story is a code. "Egypt" is a code word for the human ego, for humanity's incessantly reactive, self-seeking nature. Any aspect of our nature that controls us is Egypt. It's the oldest master-slave relationship in Creation. And it takes many forms.

- We're imprisoned by the ego-based aspects of our material existence.

- We're held in bondage by our reactive whims and egocentric desires.

- We're enslaved by our reckless impulses.

- We're held captive by our careers, jobs, and shallow relationships.

- We're prisoners to the perceptions of others.

- We're incarcerated by our ego's need for other people to accept us.

- We're hostages to our constant need to outdo our friends.

Our ego is our true taskmaster—and the ego is so good at doing its job that most of us don't even realize we are in bondage.

Accountability

As long as they were slaves in Egypt, the Israelites were not accountable or responsible for their own lives. They could remain victims. They did not have to accept blame for any suffering they experienced. It's much easier to be a victim—a slave—than to accept responsibility for life's problems.

This *victim mind-set* was the real slavery in Egypt. The exodus of the Israelites led them to genuine freedom and control over their own fate. But with freedom comes responsibility, and that was uncomfortable to a people who'd been slaves for centuries. This is the spiritual meaning behind their sudden complaints and their desire to return to Egypt. It was much easier for the Israelites to be slaves and to blame everything on the Egyptians. That way, negative events were simply beyond their control.

The truth is that no event is beyond our control. But our reactive nature blinds us to this freedom. Yet if we can accept this

responsibility, we can have the power of freedom and control
over the cosmos.

Abstaining from Bread

During the eight days of Passover, regular bread is replaced by
matzah, which is unleavened bread. The kabbalists teach us
that bread is a powerful tool. Bread is like an antenna for trans-
mitting spiritual energy, which explains its use in the rituals of
so many religions.

Kabbalah teaches that bread is also metaphysically linked to
the human ego. Just as bread has the power to expand and
rise, our ego has the ability to expand, motivating us to rise to
great heights in the material world.

Since *matzah* is unleavened, it is bread without ego—bread
whose selfish nature has been removed. By eating *matzah* with
the proper kabbalistic meditation and intentions, we receive
the power to shut down our own ego. In this way, we can free
ourselves from slavery and rise to great spiritual heights.

Bread also attracts overwhelming energy into the home. For
this reason, not even one crumb of leavened bread is eaten
during Passover, when this energy infusion reaches ultra-high
levels. Consider this example: You're driving a car at thirty
miles per hour. If you roll down the window, the sudden change
in air pressure is minimal. You can still control the vehicle. But
if you're flying in a 747 at 500 miles per hour, the tiniest crack
in a window would send the plane careening out of control.
Passover is like flying at the speed of light that's how intense

the Light of freedom is. Even the tiniest speck of bread in your system would constitute a crack in your spiritual window, sending you and your reactive behavior on a wild collision course with chaos throughout the upcoming year.

Ten Plagues

The biblical story speaks of ten plagues that were unleashed upon Egypt when Moses was securing freedom for the Israelites. The ancient kabbalists explained that the story of the ten plagues really means that ten blasts of energy are required to wipe out the ten levels of negativity that dwell within our human nature. Kabbalists also observe that reality consists of ten dimensions, each of which is expressed in our own spiritual make-up. One implication of this principle is that our ego corresponds to ten grades of spiritual negativity. Once the ten levels of negativity are removed, we achieve genuine freedom from the ego and the self.

All the compelling secrets and mysteries behind the rites and rituals of Passover are fully revealed in the book, *The Kabbalah Connection.*

Time Code

According to the Hebrew calendar, the first night of Passover opens a unique window of opportunity in the universe. The prison door is suddenly unlocked, and we have the chance to escape from the prison of our ego, fear, and insecurities. This opening was actually created some 3300 years ago when the Israelites were freed from slavery on this date. Freedom was granted to the Israelites in Egypt for one purpose: to create a reservoir of energy for all future generations, so that we could all access the power of freedom in our own lives.

Modern physics tells us that energy is never destroyed. The same spiritual energy of freedom that was made available so long ago returns every year on Passover night. This happens because time is like a revolving wheel. Events do not pass us by like a one-way freight train; we revisit the same moments each year as the wheel of time spins. The only things that change from one year to the next are the set decorations that give us the illusion of a new year and a different life.

When Passover arrives, that ancient energy of freedom is once again ours for the taking. All we have to do is connect with it.

The Forty-Nine Days of the *Omer*

Immediately after the first night of Passover, the kabbalist begins counting the *Omer*, a period of forty-nine days during which we are building a Vessel within our being so that we can receive the Light of Immortality. This Light will be revealed to us after the Counting, during the connection known as *Shavuot*. The number forty-nine is taken from the seven *Sefirot* (corresponding to seven weeks) and their seven subsections (days in the week). When we build a Vessel during the Counting of the *Omer*, we are also earning the Light we received during Passover. The Light of Freedom that we captured on Passover is considered to be a free gift, and by Counting the *Omer* we are building a Vessel to retain it.

During the *Omer*, there is very little spiritual Light available in the cosmos. This can be a dramatic change from Passover, which features an intense infusion of energy. The word *Omer* means *precise* and *little*, indicating the scarcity of spiritual energy during this time. For this reason, kabbalists do not shave or cut their hair during these forty-nine days. As we discussed earlier, hair is a powerful antenna that draws energy. Thus, we leave our hair as long as possible during the *Omer* so that we can capture the few sparks of Light that are available during that time.

The Thirty-Third Day of *Omer* (*Lag Ba'Omer*)

Although the *Omer* is a time of diminished Light, there is one day during this period that is supremely powerful. The thirty-third day of the *Omer* is one of the most powerful and important days of the year, yet it remains the least known of all the connections made available to us annually.

The thirty-third day of the *Omer* is the day when Kabbalist Rav Shimon Bar Yochai left this physical reality. Rav Shimon Bar Yochai, one of the greatest souls to ever walk this earth, is the author of the *Zohar*. Kabbalah teaches that the day of his death is important because when people leave this world, on that day all the spiritual energy and Light that they revealed throughout the course of their lives is released into the cosmos. In Rav Shimon Bar Yochai's case, he revealed no less than the Light of the *Zohar*, which, as we previously learned, embodies all the Light of Immortality that was lost on Mount Sinai. This means that the complete Light of Revelation was again released into the cosmos on the day Rav Shimon left this world.

Kabbalists also say that the pool of energy generated by a person during life becomes accessible again each year on the anniversary of his or her passing. Therefore, the thirty-third day of the *Omer* offers us nothing less than the full power of Revelation on Mount Sinai, and the power of Immortality!

Because this day is so powerful, the force called Satan has diminished its importance so that 99 percent of the world has no idea of its existence. It is a law of the universe that if an individual does not know when a given portion of energy or Light is released into the universe, he or she receives no benefit from it. That is why Satan has worked so hard to keep this day, and its true importance, a secret.

The Revelation (*Shavuot*)

After the forty-nine days of the *Omer* have passed, the connection known as *Shavuot* arrives. *Shavuot* is the day when Moses and the Israelites experienced Revelation on Mount Sinai thirty-four centuries ago. Every year on this date, the full Revelation returns to the cosmos in a state of potential. During this connection, the kabbalist stays up all night reading select verses from every Torah portion as prescribed by the renowned Kabbalist Rav Isaac Luria (the Ari). This action, along with other prayer-connections, serves to awaken and ignite the Light of Immortality.

As mentioned previously, according to the *Zohar*, sleep is one-sixtieth of death. By fighting and overcoming the body's desire to sleep, we are overpowering the Angel of Death, thereby releasing the forces of Immortality into the world. Kabbalists tell us that whoever successfully stays awake all night on *Shavuot* is guaranteed life until the next *Rosh Hashanah*.

The 9th of *Av*

Approximately 2500 years ago, the Babylonians destroyed the Holy Temple in Jerusalem. The date of the destruction was the ninth day of the Hebrew month of *Av*.

Two thousand years ago, the Romans destroyed the Second Temple in Jerusalem. The entire city was sacked, the slaughter reportedly so widespread that the cobblestone streets were knee-deep in blood. The date of the destruction and massacre was the 9th of *Av*.

In 1096, Pope Urban II launched the Crusades, in which tens of thousands of Jews and Muslims were butchered. The date was the 9th of *Av*.

In 1290, King Edward I expelled the Jews from England. The date was the 9th of *Av*.

In 1492, the Jews were expelled from Spain. King Ferdinand's deadline for expulsion or death was the 9th of *Av*. Christopher Columbus was supposed to set sail for the New World on that day, but he made his crew sit on the boat all day, waiting for that day to pass. Columbus launched his journey on the 10th of *Av*.

On August 1, 1914, Germany declared war on Russia, officially launching World War I. The date was the 9th of *Av*.

Nazi Heinrich Himmler presented the plan for the genocide of European Jewry and the Final Solution on the 9th of *Av*.

The kabbalists tell us that the 9th of *Av* is the one day of the year when the force called Satan (our Adversary) rules for the entire twenty-four-hour period. Remember that the force called Satan is not a demon or a devil but a negative force of consciousness whose sole nature is receiving, chaos, selfishness and space. This adversarial entity, the source of the human ego, was created to test and challenge humankind so that our transformation from selfish to selfless would be difficult and challenging, thus ensuring that we truly earn our place in paradise.

We have the free will to either gratify or resist the egocentric desires and reactive impulses that ignite within us twenty-four hours a day. When we allow this force to rule our consciousness, we create space between ourselves and other people which in turn creates space and disconnection between us and the World of Light. Our individual and collective behavior determines how much darkness and destruction permeate our lives and this world. If we choose to gratify our selfish desires, the eventual result will be great destruction.

On the 9th of *Av*, the force of Satan is given full reign over the universe. This is the day Satan seeks to enter into our body and mind. For this reason, on the 9th of *Av* we fast for the entire twenty-four-hour period. On this day, we abstain from all food and drink since it is tainted with his energy. We also read from the ancient biblical scroll of Lamentations (*Megilat Eicha*), written by the prophet Jeremiah to recount the story of the destruction of the Temple. Why speak of destruction on this the most destructive date in history? The reading of the scroll serves as a vaccination against the very disease that caused the destruction in the first place.

Reading this scroll and fasting will keep us completely separate from the force and consciousness of Satan, thereby empowering us with the ability to defeat this reactive consciousness throughout the entire year. Performed properly, the technology designated for this day gives us the ability to eradicate Satan from human existence for good.

Kabbalists tell us that this monumental day of destruction is also the day on which the Messiah (*Mashiach*) will be born. From the greatest darkness will emerge the greatest ray of Light. The Messiah is not a person coming to save us. Rather, the Messiah is a global state of consciousness in which humanity is freed from all reactive forms of consciousness. This state of consciousness will allow us to achieve personal freedom and eternal happiness. When a critical mass of people achieves this inner state of Messiah, this consciousness will rule all humankind and immortality and eternal pleasure will become the new reality. A global Messianic figure will arrive as a sign— not as a savior—and a seal that humankind has finally achieved the ultimate goal: the creation of heaven on Earth.

Love Connection (*Tu B' Av*)

On the fifteenth day of the Hebrew month *Av* (the astrological sign of Leo), the energy of soul mates and love permeates the cosmos. Making a connection to this day helps us to attract our true soul mate, or strengthen our existing relationship. All forms of love—for soul mates, friends, parents, children, siblings and everyone else—are strengthened on this powerful day.

Rav Yehuda Brandwein, the renowned kabbalist who taught my father, said that on this day both the sun and moon are equal in Light and shine together. This is a profound statement on many levels. Everything we perceive in this physical reality is a reflection of spiritual reality. The sun, moon, stars, mountains, oceans, and the seven continents are merely shadows and reflections of forces of consciousness in spiritual reality. The sun corresponds to the Light of the Creator and the will to share unconditionally, and the moon corresponds to the Vessel. Just as the moon has no light of its own, the Vessel is lightless but for the Light it receives from the Creator.

Rav Ashlag reveals a profound kabbalistic secret which, he says, serves as the key to grasping kabbalistic wisdom. This concept is called the Law of Affinity or the Law of Attraction. This law states that *like attracts like.* In other words, two similar things naturally gravitate to one another; while dissimilarity creates distance and space between entities. This principle contains the secret to finding your soul mate as well as to attaining biological immortality. Let's examine how.

The Light of the Creator is a sharing force; the Vessel is a receiving force. These are polar opposites. Whereas the Light is in a realm of immortality, the Vessel finds itself in a realm of death. The Light is in a world of unending order and happiness. The Vessel, because of its receiving nature, is in a world of unending chaos and sadness. Our receiving for ourselves alone (the Adversary) is the *Cause* of all our chaos because it creates distance between us and the Source of true happiness and life.

This truth is reflected within human relationships. When a man and woman only receive, when governed by their egos, they are disconnected from the Light and the two halves of one soul cannot find one another in order to connect to the 99 Percent. They've created distance between themselves and the Light, and thus between each other. But when a man and woman transform their inner nature from receiving into sharing, they are drawn to find their true soul mate so that they can unite to create one complete soul and thus connect to the Light. In other words, the closer one draws to the Light the closer one draws to his or her own soul mate for the purpose of connecting to that Light. *Like attracts like*: it's automatic.

This truth is also reflected in the state of humankind. Humankind is governed by the Adversary, which is base self-interest, the *Desire to Receive for the Self Alone*. Each person on Earth is concerned with his or her own welfare first. Consequently, the entire planet is governed by the consciousness of receiving, which is the opposite of—and therefore separated from—the positive sharing force of Light. This is why there is no lasting spiritual Light on Earth.

But when a critical mass of humanity genuinely transforms, eradicating self-interest and igniting an unconditional *Desire to Share* with others, there will be affinity and similarity between humankind and the Creator. Both will be in a positive sharing state. Accordingly, the two realities will be identical; and because like attracts like the 1 Percent and the 99 Percent will be attracted to each other. Each person on Earth will then receive the Light of the Creator for the sole purpose of sharing it with others so that an individual's act of receiving will function as an act of sharing. Humankind will be identical to the Creator (who only shares), and the Light of the Creator will flow into this world unceasingly due to the Law of

Attraction (*like attracts like*), thereby bringing about the end of death—forever.

One day the same shall occur on all levels of existence, and paradise will be our home. When we share with others unconditionally we are one with the Creator. Humankind, originally a receiver, will be a sharer, identical with the Creator, and the moon will shine as brightly as the sun.

This ancient secret is demonstrated in another way that we can interpret through kabbalistic astrology. As mentioned above, this love connection occurs in the Hebrew month *Av*, which is ruled by the astrological sign of Leo. It is interesting to note that Leo is the only sign of the Zodiac controlled by the Sun. The *Tu B'Av* love connection just happens to take place directly in the middle of the month, when the moon is complete and full.

The kabbalists tell us that when humankind completely transforms mere receiving into *Receiving for the Sake of Sharing*, our receiving action will actually be sharing and we will become identical to the Creator.

From the perspective of the spiritual cosmos, this is the only time when both the sun and the moon are in a ruling position, equal in their power and influence. Here we have the perfect expression of a genuine soul mate relationship and a direct reflection of the age of the Messiah, when immortality will rule.

part six

general ways of the kabbalist

Connecting to the Righteous Of History

As we have learned, when a person leaves this world all the spiritual Light and power that he or she revealed in life is released into the cosmos on the day of his or her death. When a righteous kabbalistic sage departs, the Light that is released is unimaginably powerful. There are a number of ways that we can tap into this Light and use it to transform our own lives. One way is to stay up all night studying the *Zohar* on the anniversary of the sage's passing. This connects us to the sage's soul and energy, drawing Light into our own lives, and infusing the entire world with Divine Energy as well.

The second way to connect to the soul of the Righteous is to light a memorial candle in the sage's name on the anniversary of his or her death. The simple flicker of a candle may look insignificant in our 1 Percent physical world, but in the 99 Percent Realm of true reality it shines brighter than a billion blazing galaxies. This incalculable infusion of Light permeates our homes when we light the memorial candle.

Another way in which we can connect to the Righteous at any time of the year is to visit their sacred gravesites. Upon their merit, the Righteous have opened up a window for us so we can connect ourselves to their souls and to the World of Light. Most of the sacred gravesites are in Israel, Ukraine, Poland and Morocco. Some of the most potent gravesites include:

- Rav Shimon Bar Yochai—Meron, Israel

- Rav Isaac Luria—Safed, Israel

- Rabbi Akiva—Tiberius, Israel

- Rabbi Yochanan Ben Zakkai—Tiberius, Israel

- The Baal Shem Tov—Medzhybizh, Ukraine

- The tombs of Abraham, Isaac, and Jacob—Hebron, Israel

- Rav Yosi of the *Zohar*—Tiberius, Israel

- Rav Chiyah of the *Zohar*—Tiberius, Israel

- The Seer of Lublin—Lublin, Poland

One unique method for using the power of the righteous souls is to *borrow* Light and energy on their merit. We can ask their assistance and request miracles upon their merit and their great name. Countless miracles occur every year in the lives of people who summon the souls of the Righteous or visit their gravesites.

The War Room

Most people throughout history have considered the synagogue to be a place of worship and prayer. The commonly held notion is that when we are in a synagogue we are praying to God, offering praises, thanks, and supplications. We are there to become more holy, righteous and pious. According to the kabbalist, nothing could be further from the truth. God does not need or want our praise, thanks or supplications. The synagogue is a

War Room. It is a command post in a spiritual battle, designed specifically to help us uproot the Adversary inside us once and for all and to bring about the death of death itself.

Rav Yehuda Ashlag, who founded The Kabbalah Centre in Jerusalem in 1922, clearly stated that whoever uses the Torah and synagogue for self-righteousness causes the Torah to become *the drug of death.* According to this great kabbalist, the Torah and synagogue, if misused, will either bring destruction and darkness to the world, or, if used properly, the death of the Angel of Death and the ignition of our Final Redemption. The consciousness of the individual determines which power the Torah unleashes.

The Separation in the War Room (*Mechitzah*)

In the War Room, there is a divider that splits the room in half. On the right side of it sit the men, and on the left side sit the women. The kabbalist sets up the partition between men and women because once again the technology of the Three Column System is at work here. This technology must be implemented in order to allow the Torah to reveal Light unto the world.

The men, on the right side of the War Room, correspond to the positive pole of a light bulb. The women on the left side correspond to the negative pole. As noted, the partition is the filament between the two, creating resistance and the consequent Light. This separation only occurs during the prayer-connections, when Divine current is flowing into the War Room.

Wearing White

People used to believe that the seven colors of the rainbow were individual colors, each with its own separate existence. Newton changed all that by shining white sunlight through a prism, revealing that the seven colors of the spectrum are actually part of white light. Newton got this idea from the *Zohar*, which he studied intently.

Thus, kabbalists understood 1500 years before Newton that white sunlight contains and includes all the colors of the spectrum. This is why men wear white clothing during the Sabbath and on the major holiday connections. White light represents the unification of all the colors and dimensions of reality. During the Sabbath and holiday connections, the underlying purpose is to unify all reality, our World of Darkness with the World of Light. By wearing white, even our clothing reflects this unified state of consciousness and helps to strengthen our connection.

Mezuzah

As we have seen, a seed precedes every fruit tree. The seed determines the quality of the tree that arises from it. Human life works the same way. Rather than running around pruning branches all day, a kabbalist always tries to transform the seeds of his or her reality. If you fix a problem at the seed level, you've affected a permanent cure. If all you do is remedy symptoms, then you're constantly coping with a problem that will never go away. Unfortunately, the force called Satan knows this and is always lurking at the seed level, waiting for an opportunity to take control of our lives.

Physical buildings operate on the same principle, and the seed of a house and all of its rooms is the doorway. To transform the negative influences that hover around the doorway of our home, Kabbalists affix a *Mezuzah* to the right door post. A *Mezuzah* is a piece of parchment inscribed with special verses and Names of God. These inscriptions have the power to polarize negative energy and transform it into positive energy.

A lot of precise work is put into the creation of a *Mezuzah*. If it is not constructed properly by a trained scribe, it will be powerless. The parchment is placed in a case made of silver, wood, or some other special materials. The case is then fastened to the right-hand side of the doorway, to ignite positive Right Column energy.

Beards and Sideburns

Male kabbalists keep some measure of a beard at all times, hair being a powerful antenna for spiritual current. The hair attracts what is known as the Light of Mercy, which protects us and helps keep judgments at bay. The hair on the head corresponds to the Right Column, a man's beard corresponds to the Left Column, and the Sideburns are the expression of the Central Column. This creates a circuit of Light so that we are in balance, filled with a constant flow of spiritual energy.

Writing the Torah

The path of Torah is designed to remove our blinders, uproot the ego, and throw a spotlight on the Satan within us so that we can eradicate his influence in our lives. Thus, there is a commandment that every person must *write* a complete Torah. The actual writing of the Torah transforms our character by infusing us with enough Light to fully expose Satan.

However, most of us are not scribes and it takes more than a year to produce a complete Torah scroll. Kabbalah explains that *writing* the Torah and *studying* the Torah can also be understood as *living* the Torah. In other words, if we use the Torah and the way of the kabbalist as part of our path in life, and we achieve a certain measure of transformation thereby, that is considered *writing* a Torah. The most powerful way to *write* a Torah is to donate a Torah through a charitable financial contribution. Charity—especially when you give till it hurts (because the only one who is really hurt by giving is Satan)—is a powerful tool for transformation. When that charity is directed toward the creation of a complete Torah scroll, it's as if the contributor *wrote* the entire Torah by his or her own hand.

Rolling Naked in the Snow

Kabbalist Rav Isaac Luria recommended rolling naked in the snow to remove any negative blockages that have been created as a result of selfish sex. Selfish sex takes place when we put our own needs ahead of those of our partner. Sex has the power to unify the spiritual and physical worlds and infuse our lives with Light. But the only way to activate this union is when our body and soul are focused on sharing instead of receiving. Prior to Kabbalah, most of us engage in sexual relations for our own pleasure. These past selfish encounters create blockages that gradually diminish the passion and energy in our sexual relationships. If we remove the blockages, we reignite the sexual energy in our relationship.

Remember, the Light is always there. The passion never left. If you want the light back, all you have to do is remove the curtains. The *Way of the Kabbalist* offers us the tools to pull back the curtains in our lives. Rolling in the snow stark naked just happens to remove a heck of a lot of curtains at one time.

Water, according to Kabbalah, is one of the substances on Earth that most closely resembles the essence of the Light of the Creator, which is why water is used for both physical and spiritual purification. Water in the form of snow is a very powerful cleansing tool. It removes lifetimes of selfish sexual acts that have created enough curtains to throw any life into shadow.

Here are some instructions for this practice, along with ancient kabbalistic meditations that we should scan before we roll. However, please note that this is not something you want to do without the support of a trained Kabbalistic instructor. Before attempting this on your own, please contact 1 800 Kabbalah to get the support and information you'll need.

Bring along a towel and a warm blanket with you, for afterward. Before rolling in the snow, meditate upon the following kabbalistic passage from the writings of Rav Isaac Luria.

1. Scan the following:

Meditation

מִי שֶׁמִּתְגַּלְגֵּל ט' גִּלְגּוּלִים, יְכַוֵּין לְיַחֵד וּלְחַבֵּר ט' אוֹתִיּוֹת שֶׁל ג' הַיָּ"ה דֹּגַ' אֲהֹיָ"ה הֵנּוּ', שֶׁהֵם סוֹד ו"ת שֶׁל ג' פַּרְצוּפִים הַנּוֹכָר, עִם אַלְפִין שֶׁבְּשֶׁלְשֶׁע רָאשׁוֹנוֹת שֶׁלָהֶם, הֲרֵי ט'.

2. Lie face-down in the snow and then roll nine times,
each roll starts and ends face down. The most effective
way to roll is in units of three.

Tithing

There are ten dimensions of true reality. Seven dimensions
affect us directly, which is why there are seven colors of the
rainbow and seven days of the week. But complete reality consists of ten dimensions. Our material world is the tenth dimension, the domain of the Adversary, Satan, the force called ego.
Our world represents 10 percent of total reality, so everything
contains at least 10 percent negative energy.

Kabbalists always tithe 10 percent of their income—no more
and no less—not as charity, but as a tool to rid our livelihood of
the force called Satan. Tithing cuts Satan out of our lives and
ensures that blessings and sustenance will continue to flow to
us. If we do not tithe, we have literally given the negative force
a piece of our income and a window through which to enter.
Tithing slams the window shut. When we tithe, we wind up
making more money. If we retain that 10 percent, the force of
Satan winds up extracting an even greater payment from us
over the long term.

Any money contributed in addition to the 10 percent tithe is considered an act of free-will charity.

Nails

The human fingernail is made of a material that has enormous spiritual power. Adam's original immortal body, prior to physical creation and the Fall of Adam, was made of a substance very similar to the fingernail. After the sin, Adam (humanity) took physical form and all that was left of his original immortal body were the nails on his ten fingers and ten toes, corresponding to the ten *Sefirot*. Our nails are one of the few links we have left to immortality, which is why nails keep growing back after they are cut, while limbs of the body do not.

Cut nails left out in the open attract all the negative forces in the universe that seek to derive nourishment from the spiritual Light in those nails. The cut nail becomes a connection to death, the opposite of immortality. When we cut our nails, it's important to dispose of them by burning them. Fallen nails on the ground are extremely negative. According to the ancient kabbalists, if pregnant women step on cut nails it can cause miscarriages. For this reason, great care must be taken to dispose of them right away. It's also important to keep nails clean and manicured in order to tap their full power.

Wine, Bread, and Salt

Wine is a tool we use to bridge the spiritual and physical realities. Wine works like a cable that conducts spiritual current into our reality. This is why wine has the power to make us giddy and drunk with happiness. When wine is used as a cable and conduit to manifest Light in our world and our bodies, it illuminates us with balanced energy. However, if we use wine for other purposes, such as self-indulgent drinking not connected to a spiritual purpose, that same energy can become destructive, which is the spiritual cause of alcoholism.

Wine is considered Left Column energy because of its ability to receive and attract energy, like the negative pole in a bulb. Water is Right Column energy, so every time we open a new bottle of red wine we pour a drop of water in to balance it. Then we recite a blessing-connection over the wine, which instills the Central Column energy of resistance. Now the wine possesses a complete inner energy structure, allowing it to operate as a conduit to transfer the energy of the spiritual world into our physical bodies.

As we've seen, bread is also a conduit that conducts a tremendous amount of energy. When we eat bread to draw energy, we dip the first piece in salt. Salt emanates from the spiritual dimension known as *Chochmah*, which allows us to connect to the positive aspect of the bread. To eat bread without injecting the Light of *Chochmah* and a blessing is to connect only to the Left Column force of receiving, which creates a short circuit. Salt's metaphysical basis in *Chochmah* is the reason it enlivens bland food, because salt injects sparks of Light into everything it touches. This takes place on the spiritual level, but on the physical level we experience it as improved *taste*.

Money

Money, according to Kabbalah, is a powerful metaphysical force that transcends our traditional view of it as a merely physical commodity. Money is a reflection of the intangible Light of the Creator. Money's energy is not derived from its physical essence or its materiality. Its value resides in the realm of human consciousness.

Money is the positive Right Column force, and our desire for it corresponds to the Left Column force of receiving. Thus, money that is used solely to enrich one's own life eventually causes darkness, because positive and negative are connecting without a filament in between. This is why often you see so much chaos in the lives of the wealthy. Kids on drugs. Suicide. Anxiety. Disease. All these kinds of tragedies are a manifestation of this type of short circuit.

Charity and tithing are two ways in which we integrate the filament in our money bulb. By resisting the *Desire to Receive* money selfishly, and instead sharing it with others in need we incorporate the Central Column force of resistance. This ensures that Light constantly shines in our life—and, believe it or not, this also ensures a constant flow of money in our lives. That is the paradox: the more we share, the more we receive. Only the Adversary blinds us to this truth.

This is why there is so much poverty in the world. The Adversary is controlling all the money by controlling the consciousness of the people. If all people—wealthy, middle class and lower class—shared a portion of their money to the point of hurting the ego, miracles would unfold in the world. That power of inner

transformation would banish death and chaos from human existence. But the Adversary makes us doubt that truth because
that is the one weapon that would destroy him forever.

Money was originally based on gold and silver coins.
Thousands of years ago, the kabbalists told us that silver is the
manifestation of the Right Column, and gold is the manifestation of the Left Column. When we share and exchange money
with others, our consciousness should be to make a fair deal
and help the other person obtain what he or she needs.
Likewise, the other person's consciousness should be directed
toward fulfilling our needs. This kind of sharing consciousness
injects the Central Column force of resistance into our transactions, ensuring that the money we use is filled with Light and
bringing Light into the rest of our lives. If we exchange money
and goods for the sole sake of our own selfish profit, there is no
circuitry in our money. Darkness will inevitably appear somewhere in our lives down the road.

The transactions remain the same. It's the consciousness
behind the transactions that determines whether money generates Light for everyone or merely a temporary burst of pleasure
followed by darkness.

Charity (*Tzedaka*)

Kabbalah says that the act of giving of money as charity is so
powerful that it can actually save someone from death. If a
decree of death has been issued upon an individual from the
universe, that person can have the decree annulled by making
a truly charitable monetary contribution.

There are different levels of charity consciousness. At the lowest level, we give, and the recipient knows who the giver is. This channel is not pure because there is some aspect of ego involved on the part of the giver, whether intentional or unintentional. At the next-highest level, the recipient does not know who the giver is, but the giver knows who the recipient is. The highest level is when the giver doesn't know who the charity is going to, and the recipient of the charity doesn't know who gave it.

Below are some insights on the power of money and charity from the ancient *Zohar*:

- The person who is generous with his money displays his belief in God that even though he shares his money with others, God is sure to give him enough to supply his needs. (*Zohar III, 110b*)

- He who has a regular charitable schedule, weekly or monthly for a fixed amount to a fixed worthy person, causes unification in the world of time and therefore can prolong his own allotted time. (*Tikkunei Zohar 58a*)

- One who has mercy on the needy is accounted as if he restored his soul, and so will his soul be restored. (*Zohar II, 198a*)

- If a harsh decree is issued against a particular individual, God many times sends him a charitable situation, and if he fulfills this obligation, the decree is nullified. (*Zohar III 110b*)

- A worthy charitable recipient should be viewed by the donor as a gift sent to him from heaven. (*Zohar II 198a*)

- He who gives charity generously is accounted as if he loaned God from his money. (*Zohar II 255a*)

- He who is generous with the needy sustains the entire world. (*Zohar I 109a*)

- Charity is called life. (*Zohar I 108*)

- Charity, if abundant enough, can effectuate changes in the laws of nature, and new cures and medicines are suddenly discovered. (*Zohar II 59a*)

The Messiah (*Mashiach*)

The kabbalistic view of the Messiah is different from the commonly held view. The Messiah is not an individual who is coming to save us. Instead, the Messiah should be understood as a state that each person can achieve within. As more and more people achieve that state, a threshold will eventually be crossed, and the entire world will transform. Then the global Messiah will appear to signify that the Redemption of humankind has taken place.

From the kabbalistic point of view, there are two Messiahs: the Messiah who is the son of Joseph, and the Messiah who is the son of David. The first Messiah is here to wage war. This is a spiritual war designed to raise and awaken free human consciousness, which is held captive to Satan (ego). It is a war waged through the dissemination of kabbalistic wisdom—the *Zohar*—which is, in essence, spiritual Light. As we attain more knowledge, we overcome our ego, which is what separates us from the Light. The more we remove what separates us, the stronger the connection. We acquire more Light. This Light rouses our consciousness so that we can perceive true reality, and enjoy the rewards of sharing and loving our neighbors.

The second Messiah, the son of David, is here to officiate and seal the peace that will erupt all over the world once the war has been won. Some kabbalists tell us that one man can be both the son of Joseph and the son of David. Other kabbalists say it will be two separate individuals. It really doesn't matter. What matters is that you and I must accept responsibility for achieving our own internal state of Messiah. Once we do, as a planet, it will not matter if one, two, or fifty-three different global Messiahs appear. All tears will have stopped flowing and the pain will be over.

Every generation has a potential global physical Messiah who can hasten the arrival of the Final Redemption by sharing the spiritual wisdom of Kabbalah with the world. He can inspire the world to embrace the universal teachings of spirituality, the *Zohar* and Kabbalah so that more and more people will understand and embrace the work necessary to end darkness and death in our world. Yet it always remains the responsibility of the individual to establish his or her own connection and relationship with the Light of the Creator.

Kabbalah says the Messiah (both the global and the personal Messiah) must enter into the darkest corners of human existence as part of the process of achieving paradise in the world.

This is because one cannot transform what one does not possess. To transform darkness into Light, each of us, including the global Messiah, must attach ourselves to a measure of darkness in order to defeat it and transform it. The global Messiah, because of his great spiritual strength, will often attach himself to the largest portion of negativity in order to lighten the load of the rest of the world. Even though the global Messiah accepts this greater responsibility (knowingly or unknowingly), this in no way absolves each individual of waging his or her own internal war against the consciousness of selfishness and ego.

In fact, accepting this responsibility and becoming accountable for our darkest traits actually delivers immense blessings. For instance, each of us comes into this world with a certain type and amount of negativity. Furthermore, each of us has done things that we are not proud of during the course of our lives. We have behaved selfishly and have committed a number of negative actions, some minor, some major. The moment we embrace the way of the kabbalist and choose to change our lives and transform, all that darkness that we've created now has the potential to be converted into pure Light once we complete our transformation. The darkness is not washed away; it actually transforms into blessings! It also contributes to the spiritual welfare of the rest of the world.

For example, if you are troubled by various fears, and you defeat them and transform by using these kabbalistic tools, you weaken the force of fear (perpetuated by the Adversary) on a global scale. Every person on Earth will have his or her own fears diminished because of your singular effort. Or, if you are an abusive individual and you use these tools to genuinely transform, you weaken the global influence of Satan so that all people in the world will be less abusive to others. We are all connected with one another. As other people transform, their efforts benefit us, and vice versa. If enough people take up the challenge of walking in the way of the kabbalist, the transformation of our world can be sped up exponentially.

All the sins of humankind, all the darkness and vile behavior of which humans are capable, are the manifestation of the Adversary within us. That's the bad news. The good news is, because he is in us, we can defeat him. Being born with negative traits is like being born into a boxing ring with your opponent for the heavyweight championship of the world. To win the championship belt, you need to put on your gloves and fight. Likewise, to defeat the Adversary, we need to put on our gloves. Our negative traits are the opponent. The boxing ring is our consciousness. The battle takes place in the mind, which controls all of our behavior.

So instead of feeling guilty about our negative thoughts, desires and traits, we need to get busy fighting them and transforming them so that they are converted into blessings, positive energy and pure Light. This is the meaning of Messiah. We are our own saviors. God gave us all the tools necessary to achieve our own salvation. The *Zohar*, the source of the Light that was lost on Mount Sinai, is the greatest weapon we have to manifest our own personal Messiah—and, in turn, the global Messiah.

As more and more *Zohars* are spread throughout the world, we wage war against the Adversary more and more effectively. Thus, the greatest act of charity and enlightened greed that a person can perform is to donate *Zohars* to as many people as possible. This is the best way to hasten the arrival of the Messiah.

Geniza

It is forbidden to erase or throw away any written Hebrew Name of God. Thus, kabbalists have created the *Geniza*, a depository where people can place documents that contain the Names of God that are no longer in a condition to be used. These include old holy books, prayer books, meditation cards, calendars, or Torah scrolls that are falling apart or have become outdated, *Tefillin* or *Tzitzit* that are defective; or unwanted pieces of paper that have Holy words on them. When the depository is full, it is taken to a special place and buried.

Sage and Incense

During the time of the Second Temple in Jerusalem more than twenty centuries ago, sage and various blends of incense were lit to remove negative influences from the environment. The *Zohar* tells us that under the right circumstances, incense can be powerful enough to remove the force of death itself. Today, we light incense and sage in our homes to purify them and help remove darkness from our lives.

The *Zohar* explains that each of the two human nostrils serves a distinct spiritual function. One nostril brings the spiritual essence of air to the brain, while the other nostril delivers the spiritual essence of air to the heart. The brain is the seat of our intelligence, and the heart is the source of our emotions. Thus, incense entering into the nose can bring balance and unification between the emotions and the intellect, helping ensure that our actions are both wise and loving. Sage and incense should be lit prior to the Sabbath. As you carry the incense into every room of your home, recite the 42-letter Name of God to strengthen the cleansing and purification process.

Special incenses are available at any of the worldwide Kabbalah Centres.

Astrology

We do not study kabbalistic astrology so we can learn how to draw up people's horoscopes. On the contrary, the purpose of kabbalistic astrology is to rise above the influences of the cosmos and take control over our own lives.

The twelve signs of the Zodiac correspond to the twelve tribes of Israel, the twelve months of the year, and the twelve permutations of the four-letter Name of God, known as the Tetragrammaton. The Zodiac sign in which we are born transmits to us all the negative and positive traits that we will need to effect our own transformation. However, the signs of the Zodiac are *not* the Cause of our personality traits; they are the *Effect*. Our karma from previous lives determines which sign we need to be born under in order to acquire the necessary traits and attributes that will allow us to correct and transform previous negative activity. The Zodiac is merely the mechanism that the soul uses to ensure that particular qualities are infused into it at birth.

The patriarch Abraham was the first kabbalistic astrologer, some 3800 years ago. He wrote a book known as *Sefer Yetzira*, the *Book of Formation*. Contained within it are all of the secrets of the universe, including the knowledge of astrology and cosmology.

As we delve into kabbalistic astrology, right away we find one significant difference between it and conventional astrology: kabbalistic astrology uses different calendars. While conventional astrology is based on the solar or Gregorian calendar, kabbalistic astrology uses the Hebrew calendar, which takes into account the positions of both the sun and the moon.

In order to determine what your astrological sign is in the Hebrew calendar, you can visit the following Web site: www.hebcal.com/converter. You may find that you have a different sign in the Hebrew calendar from the one you have in the Gregorian calendar.

Each month, we have the ability to take control over the astrological influences of the month (see The Head of the Month, on page 121). This is because each month is controlled by two Hebrew letters that function like astrological DNA. One letter controls the sign that rules that month; the other letter controls the planet that rules the month. Meditating upon these letters at the head of the month is one way to take control of the consciousness of that month.

Numerology (*Gematria*)

Each letter of the Hebrew alphabet has a specific numerical value. The reason for this is to allow the letters to communicate additional knowledge, insight, and information regarding the meanings of words and phrases. The most basic form of numerology involves adding up the numerical values of each letter in a particular word. When you know the numerical value of a word, you know more about its meaning on both the mundane and the spiritual levels.

Words that share the same value have a spiritual connection with one another. These connections can provide valuable insights into the true nature of reality. For instance, the numerical value of the Hebrew word for "snake" (*nachash*) is 358, which is the same as that for the Hebrew word for "Messiah" (*Mashiach*). The snake, of course, refers to the snake or serpent in the Garden of Eden that seduced Adam and Eve. The snake is Satan. Thus, kabbalists tell us that from the ultimate form of darkness (snake) will emerge the ultimate illumination of Light (Messiah). This is why "snake" and "Messiah" have a numerological connection. This interconnection also tells us that each of us has a portion of the snake infused into our nature. When we defeat and transform this negative nature, we attain our own personal state of Messiah within.

Let us look at another example. The word for the World of Light, the 99 Percent Reality, is the sacred and most famous Name of God—the Tetragrammaton—referred to by the letters *Yud*, *Hei*, *Vav*, and *Hei*.

This particular Name of God has a numerical value of 26. Interestingly, we *never* pronounce this Name of God. Rather, we utter a different Name of God whenever we come across the Tetragrammaton in a prayer-connection book. The Name of God we utter instead of the Tetragrammaton is *Adonai* אֲדֹנָי Why do we read one word but recite another one? *Adonai* pertains to our 1 Percent physical reality. By visually connecting with the Name of God that refers to the Spiritual World and then uttering the Name of God that refers to our physical dimension, we join and connect the two realities so that energy and Light fill the Earth.

The Name of God that correlates to our physical dimension— *Adonai*—has a numerical value of 65. When our physical world (*Adonai* = 65) connects with the spiritual realm (*Tetragrammaton* = 26), the numerical values of both Names of God add up to 91. And it so happens that the Hebrew word "*amen*," recited after a prayer connection is made, has the numerical value of 91. Saying "*amen*" unifies the two Names of God connecting the physical world with the spiritual world. Also, if you add up the digits that produce 91 (9 + 1) the sum is 10, corresponding to the ten *Sefirot* (dimensions), which are now all connected as one.

Remarkably, much of the world has been saying "*amen*" for millennia, never knowing that the power of this word is based on the wisdom of Kabbalah.

These are just a few examples of how numerology lends additional insights into the words and phrases associated with biblical wisdom. Words and phrases that look religious, mythical, ritualistic, or just plain nonsensical can actually open their deep meanings to you when you understand the numerical values that lie within them.

Angels

Angels are not sweet-faced winged cherubs that flutter about like fireflies. Angels constitute a metaphysical communication system that transfers energy from one realm to another. They are a conduit between the physical reality and the spiritual dimension. Just as we cannot plug a toaster directly into a hydroelectric turbine, we cannot connect directly to the awesome energy that permeates the World of Light. Angels are the two-way communication system that grants us access to that energy. They carry our prayers to the world of Light, and they carry Light from that world to ours.

We can connect to angels in a variety of ways. Each day of the week, there are Angels (i.e., influences) of the Day that allow us to tap into positive energy. We connect to the Angels of the Day by meditating upon various sequences of Hebrew letters that are the equivalent to the DNA of each angelic entity. These meditations can be found in the book, *Prayer of the Kabbalist: The 42-Letter Name of God*.

Each time we speak positive words and commit positive deeds, we literally bring a new angel into existence. As these positive influences accumulate, they help us in many ways. For instance, when we find ourselves at just the right place at the right time, it is often the positive angelic influences that have brought us there. When things just happen to go right, this, too, is attributed to the influences of the angels.

On the other hand, each time we speak negatively about others, curse, shout in anger, or commit any negative action we cause a negative influence, or angel, to come into existence. These negative influences cling to us all day long. When we are low in energy, depressed, or find things constantly going wrong, this is the result of the negative angels we've produced.

Dreams

"When a man sleeps in his bed, his soul leaves him to soar above, each soul according to its own way." — The *Zohar*

We all dream. We all have awakened in the middle of the night, consumed by images of an alternate reality. All of us have awoken terrified by a nightmare or inspired by images that bathe us in an overwhelming sense of peace and joy. In our dreams, we often witness bizarre events in strange places, under weird circumstances. Dreams have long been seen as a healing force, an extension of the waking state, and a source of divination and prophetic messages.

When we sleep, the *Zohar* tells us, a major portion of our soul leaves our body to "plug in" to the 99 Percent World of Light. Just enough of the soul is left behind to keep our bodies safe from harm. Thus, sleep is not merely a time for the body to rest;

it is a time for the soul to access the source of its power. Without this recharge provided by sleep, we become lethargic and confused. We are unable to concentrate. We become depressed. The "light" seems to have gone out of our lives.

The *Zohar* teaches us that we have all come into this world to nourish and nurture our connection to the hidden World of Light. Wouldn't it be nice if you could get periodic communications from the World of Light that reassured you when you were moving in the right direction, or warned you when you were going astray? The *Zohar* tells us that we *do* get these communications. They are called dreams.

Every dream is a message from the hidden true reality. During our waking hours a constant struggle is taking place between the physical consciousness of the body, which seeks momentary material satisfaction, and the consciousness of the soul, which aspires to the World of Light and lasting happiness. However, during sleep, this dynamic changes. Body-consciousness is released, and the soul is set free to revisit a realm beyond time and space. In this elevated state, we receive messages in the form of dreams from the profound Intelligence inhabiting this realm. When we awaken, a dream can become our own private navigational instrument, helping us plot a course through the storms of daily life. This is why every dream deserves our attention. It is important to recognize, however, that some dreams are more attached to the World of Light than others.

The *Zohar* tells us that there are several levels of dreams. Like e-mail messages, a dream may have low priority, normal priority, or high priority. Some dreams might even be categorized as junk mail (and are probably caused by eating too much junk food before bed!). And, depending on the spiritual nature of the dreamer, every dream could have some mixture of priorities within it. Even the highest-priority dream might have some junk mixed in. Dreams that take place prior to 4:00 a.m. are usually messages; dreams that take place in the early morning are often sent to confuse us.

If we are engaged in behavior that is leading us to a dangerous consequence somewhere down the road, a dream will come to warn us to change our ways. Kabbalists offer us a technique to cancel out and nullify a negative dream, which, in turn, helps shift us into an alternate universe or destiny. The *Zohar* gives us the techniques to interpret our dreams so that we can separate the junk, pull out the gems, and grasp the underlying message. Please see *The Dreams Book* to learn more about dreams and deeper insights into dream interpretation.

The *Zohar* says a dream that is not interpreted is like an important piece of mail that you fail to open.

Reincarnation

In the beginning, there was Light. The Light was not physical; it was a force of consciousness. The Light then created the vessel to receive the Light. The Vessel was not physical either, but rather a force of consciousness that would include all the conscious beings that have walked—or ever will walk—this Earth. And just as all the colors of the rainbow join together to create white light, all the various consciousnesses were united into this one giant soul or consciousness.

The nature of the Vessel was to receive. So in the beginning there was the consciousness of sharing, which was a positive-charged force of intelligence, and there was a receiving consciousness of the Vessel, a negative-charged force of intelligence. The positive consciousness created the negative consciousness. But when the Vessel was created, it also inherited the DNA of the Consciousness that created it, so the Vessel contained both a negative consciousness and a potential positive consciousness that it inherited from the Light. The Vessel also possessed free will, which was the neutral consciousness that allowed the Vessel to choose between positive and negative, sharing and receiving.

The Vessel chose to leave the perfected reality that existed prior to our physical universe in order to create its own paradise, which was really just a re-creation of the perfected reality it had once inhabited. The Vessel could create this paradise by *resisting* its innate nature to receive. Each time it resisted, the Vessel gained access to a measure of its inherited positive DNA, so the Vessel's ultimate goal was to completely resist all receiving so that the full power of its positive DNA can be unleashed.

This plan could not be carried out in the perfected world because the Vessel dwelt in God's presence and constantly received all it needed. When reality is perfect, there is nothing to resist, nothing to perfect, nothing to reveal. There is no *space*. So God created a space by withdrawing a miniscule portion of the Light. The creation of this space, this vacuum, created the Big Bang, which took place fifteen billion years ago.

The *Zohar* tells us that when God created space, the Vessel then shattered into countless fragments and sparks that scattered into this empty vacuum called space. Each piece of the broken Vessel, says the *Zohar*, contains all three forces of consciousness (positive, negative and neutral). When the Vessel's shards descended from the spiritual reality, they became more dense and thick as they moved away from their source. These sparks thickened so much that they created the illusion of matter. Then they configured and combined in a countless variety of ways, producing the entire earth, including the mineral, vegetable, and animal kingdoms—and humankind, of course.

Everything in our world is part of the original shattered Vessel. Since that original Vessel was made up of consciousness, this means that the physical world is simply consciousness in frozen form. Today physicists are telling us that atomic particles are not really physical. Their locations are not fixed, but are based on probabilities. All physicality is an illusion. The motion of atomic particles is what creates the illusion of matter, the same way that a fan's rotor spins so fast that it creates the illusion of a solid disk.

Because science uses a different word to describe the Vessel (that word being *matter*), we become confused regarding the true nature of reality. If science called the electron *Desire to Receive*, then we would understand that consciousness is the essence of reality. These words and names may cause confusion; but the kabbalist and the scientist are describing the same force.

Science tells us that matter never dies. It is immortal. In the language of Kabbalah, that would mean consciousness never dies, the Vessel never dies. Consciousness is immortal.

What dies, then, when a person leaves this world? Simply an arrangement of atoms. Think of Lego building blocks. Suppose we assemble all the Lego pieces necessary to build a man. When all the pieces are together, the man is alive. But when space comes between the Lego pieces—that is, when we disassemble them—the man is now *dead*. But the individual Lego pieces can be rearranged to build another man, or another woman. The pieces never die. What died was the particular arrangement of those pieces. This is what happens with matter. It never dies. Its components merely become separated from one another, causing our bodies to disintegrate.

When we die, the particles that made up our bodies simply circulate back into the environment. Some atoms from the deceased person can go on and bond with other atoms to produce a new tree. Other atoms may bond to create a mountain, or a zebra, or another human being.

Now, when you consider that atoms are really particles of consciousness, you can understand how reincarnation is as natural as breathing and sleeping. The human soul is just a force of consciousness. So is the human body. It's all one. Atoms are part of what constitutes both the human body and the human soul, but there are many levels to the soul, just as there are deeper levels of particles that form an atom. Kabbalah says the soul has five levels, and each of the five levels contains five levels. As science probes deeper into the atom, it is finding confirmation of the deeper levels of soul and consciousness that Kabbalah described many centuries earlier.

Atoms are made of electrons, protons and neutrons, but these subatomic particles are made of smaller particles such as leptons, quarks, bosons and gluons. Even more amazingly, science says that all of these particles are just packets of energy, vibrations that create the illusion of matter once they reach the level of atoms and molecules. If science could penetrate into every fundamental layer of exotic subatomic particles, they would continue to find tinier and tinier particles. But these are not particles like billiard balls. These are merely the sparks of the shattered Vessel, particles of consciousness that fell into our physical reality from the World of Light.

Light

This is what physicists would find if they were able to reach the most minute level of reality—an infinite, unending, luminous ocean of Light. The World of Light is within and beneath the level of atoms, electrons, quarks and gluons. At the very innermost level we find true reality. Ironically, outer space is the wrong way to heaven and paradise. Deep space is nothing but an empty, barren, dark, cold vacuum. It's the vacuum that God created when God withdrew a portion of Light to create a space for the shattered Vessel to inhabit.

Now that we know that matter is immortal and that atoms and subatomic particles are really particles of consciousness, we can understand the cycle of Creation. Atoms and their constituent particles, all of which possess consciousness, come together to create a specific human being. That human being is endowed with life. And the purpose of life is to resist selfishness and ego and unleash the Godly nature in our soul—the *Desire to Share*. This is our true nature. If we fail to achieve this transformation, this means we have spent more time reacting than being proactive. Each time we react, we inject the consciousness of *space* into our being, between the atoms that bind together to create us. When atoms stop bonding, the molecules they form fall apart, and our body begins to deteriorate. This is called aging. But really it is just *space* consciousness permeating the consciousness of our atoms.

When we reach a critical mass of reactions and egocentric behavior in our lives, the space in our atoms and our consciousness becomes so great that we die. The atoms stop bonding and fall away from one another for good. There are trillions upon trillions of atoms that produce a human being. The majority of those atoms will find their way and produce a different human being at some point in the future, in order to find the right opportunity to make a specific correction in life and transform. However, some might become part of an animal or plant.

Beneath the diversity of this physical world, there is a simple unity called matter, and the particles that make up this matter are the shards of the shattered Vessel. That Vessel was made of consciousness, which is the substance of the human soul *and* of the human body. Consciousness is the only reality. And the only battle we face is the battle against the ego consciousness of Satan whose mission is to befuddle our understanding and to make us doubt his very existence.

Particles will keep bonding and coming apart, simulating life and death, and producing new living beings, until we all complete our transformation. There is no real death, because matter is immortal. There is only space. When we say goodbye to loved ones, the space opening up between us is what hurts. When our body decays because of space entering it, it may be painful. But there is no real death. There is only space, and pain caused by the ego.

When we love another, when our consciousness is totally focused on sharing and loving unconditionally, there is no more space in our consciousness, and there will be no more space within our bodies. Matter is immortal. Once our particles stay bonded together forever, we will live forever, because the building blocks that produce us will never die.

This is the way of the kabbalist.

The Power of Study

In Kabbalah, our study is never intended to increase our intellectual prowess. We're not trying to become smarter; we're trying to become *purer*. Study is a technology that removes the ego that separate us from our soul and from the Light of the Creator.

Here's how it works: When we struggle over an idea or concept in Kabbalah, the effort of trying to understand the principle builds a Vessel within us. Light can never manifest in our physical reality unless there is a Vessel to contain it. The same way we need a glass to contain water so that we can more easily drink it, we need a container to hold the Light that fills all reality so that we can more easily ingest it. Striving to learn Kabbalah builds the Vessel.

The moment we say, "A-ha, now I understand," that is the moment when the Light fills the Vessel within us. Study is a technology. It's a mechanism for inviting the Light of the 99 Percent Realm into our 1 Percent Dimension.

This added Light automatically removes curtains, blockages, and darkness in our lives so that we become more pure. The purer we are, the more we will share. The more we share, the closer we draw to the Light, because we are becoming more similar to the Light. This brings us yet more Light and more happiness. We begin to spiral upward into ever-increasing levels of happiness and fulfillment. Studying Kabbalah sets it all in motion.

The key to making our study successful is not how much we learn, but rather how much we share and care for others during our day. If we are intolerant, abusive, or just plain nasty to people, our study is worthless. The curtains we create through our unkind actions become so thick that our study sessions cannot possibly penetrate those drapes of darkness. As long as we strive to be just a little bit nicer each day, our study sessions will work miracles.

If possible, it's good to study in groups, because each person will bring their own unique portion of Light to the session. Kabbalists often study after midnight because metaphysical windows on the hidden dimensions open up during the dark of night. The Light that is generated through late-night study permanently counterbalances the darkness and judgment that reign after the sun sets each night.

Repentance

Repentance is perhaps the most misunderstood word in all of human language. For this reason, I left this topic for the very end because it is, without doubt, also the most important. Everything discussed in this book is, in fact, encapsulated in this one specific topic, which further emphasizes the tragedy of ignorance and misconception.

Repentance does not mean saying, "I'm sorry." Repentance has nothing to do with remorse, guilt, regret or religion, as we traditionally understand these concepts. Repentance is a time-travel technology and a methodology for reattaching our world to the 99 Percent reality.

The Hebrew word for repentance (*teshuvah*) actually means to *return*. Only through the *Zohar* can we understand the meaning and power of repentance and what it has to do with the concept of *returning*. I could say with accuracy that the whole path of Kabbalah and the *Way of the Kabbalist* is about repentance. But *repentance* is a dangerously loaded word. Without a Kabbalistic understanding of this word, religious extremism, intolerance and bloodshed will inevitably result. Let's now reveal one of the deep secrets of Kabbalah that relates to repentance.

As discussed in this book, true reality consists of Ten *Sefirot*—also known as the ten dimensions—nine of which are hidden from our view. The hidden dimensions are structured as follows: The Upper Three are considered one group, and they do not directly influence our reality. The next Six Dimensions are actually fused into one super-dimension, and this is the 99

Percent Reality that we have been talking about throughout this book. This super-dimension is also referred to by the Hebrew term *Zeir Anpin*.

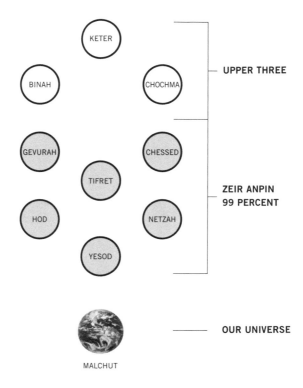

WHEN our world is connected to the six dimensions directly above it (*Zeir Anpin* or the 99 Percent), Light flows into our world. Think of our world as a lamp. If a lamp is not plugged in, it remains dark. When you plug the lamp into an electrical outlet, the lamp illuminates. The 99 Percent Realm is the wall socket that contains the electrical current we need to activate the lamp of our world.

These ten dimensions are encoded within the Tetragrammaton, or the four-letter Name of God.

As we have seen, the four Hebrew letters that compose this name are *Yud, Hei, Vav,* and *Hei* (see below).

4-LETTER NAME OF GOD

Final Hei   Vav   Hei   Yud

The very tip of the first letter of this sacred four-letter name of God, *Yud,* corresponds to the first of the ten dimensions, called *Keter.* The rest of the body that forms *Yud* corresponds to the second dimension, called *Chochmah.* The second letter, *Hei,* corresponds to the *Sefira* known as *Binah.* The third letter, *Vav,* contains six dimensions, collectively known as *Zeir Anpin* and individually called *Chesed, Gevurah, Tiferet, Netzach, Hod* and *Yesod.* And the fourth letter, *Hei,* refers to our physical reality of *Malchut* (see below).

4-LETTER NAME OF GOD

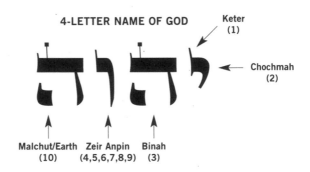

Keter (1)

Chochmah (2)

Malchut/Earth (10)   Zeir Anpin (4,5,6,7,8,9)   Binah (3)

As we have discussed, the Law of Attraction stipulates that *like attracts like*. Our world of *Malchut/Earth* is ruled by the collective consciousness of humankind. Thus, if humankind is governed by self-interest, ego, and the *Desire to Receive*, the nature of *Malchut/Earth* is now the complete opposite of *Zeir Anpin* (the 99 Percent), whose sole nature is positive sharing. Therefore, these dimensions mutually repel one another because of their opposite states of consciousness—receiving versus sharing.

This mutual repulsion causes disconnection within the Name of God. It creates repulsion between the 1 Percent and the 99 Percent. Earth disconnects from the Source of all Light. We disconnect from the Light of the Creator. There is now *space* between the World of Light and the World of Darkness (see below).

4-LETTER NAME OF GOD

Earth | Zeir Anpin/99 Percent

Disconnection Between Zeir Anpin and Malchut
Space between the 99 Percent and 1 Percent

Kabbalists talk about God's Name not being unified, but the secret meaning behind this concept is that God's Name refers to the complete structure of the *Ten Sefirot*, the true reality that includes our world. Unifying the Name of God refers to connecting the final *Hei* (*Malchut*) to the *Vav* (*Zeir Anpin*).

We accomplish this feat by removing the *Cause* that created the separation in the first place. That Cause was the human ego—a selfish character trait that motivated us to react and behave with self-interest—the opposite behavior of the 99 Percent Reality, which only shares Light. How do we remove that trait? Through *repentance*.

Remember, the Hebrew word for repentance means *to return*. To repent, we must *return* to the moment of our misdeed. We must recall and relive the event within our consciousness. In simpler terms, *returning* implies that we are recognizing that our behavior caused the space and darkness in our lives. In so doing, we are becoming accountable for our chaos. We are admitting that we alone are the Cause of all that is wrong in our lives.

Acknowledging that we are the Cause of our own problems and making the effort *to return* to the scene of the crime—a crime in which *we* are the culprit—is the most difficult feat of all. It's always so much easier to just say "I'm sorry" and move on with our lives. But that is being religious. It is not being spiritual, or smart. Saying "I'm sorry" is easier because it entails no pain on our part. There's no *payment*. Only empty words.

The purpose of *returning* to the scene of the crime is to experience the actual pain we inflicted upon the victim of our misdeed. If we truly ask the Light to allow us to feel the pain, make no mistake about it, we *will* feel some real pain. And the pain we'll feel is the pain that is now being taken away from the person that we've hurt, even if it took place decades earlier. And this shifting of pain from the victim to the culprit will restore balance in the universe.

There is a second, even more important aspect of the concept of *returning*. Now that we've *returned* to the original transgression, we can use the *Zohar*, or the Sabbath, or *Rosh Hashanah*, or any one of the many tools that the *Way of the Kabbalist* gives us, to uproot and banish the egocentric trait that caused us to behave selfishly. How does that happen? If we are sincere—genuinely, absolutely sincere—in our desire to lose that nasty trait for good, the tools of Kabbalah ignite the Light, which initiates a change within our consciousness. When you experience this change for yourself, you will feel and know the power and magic that is Kabbalah.

Now here's the amazing part: Once this negative receiving trait is eradicated, we are no longer *dissimilar* to *Zeir Anpin*, the 99 Percent Realm. The one trait that caused repulsion between ourselves and the Light no longer exists. Guess what? Now the Law of Attraction works in our favor, and we are drawn back toward the Light.

This leads us to another deep secret regarding the word repentance and the true meaning of returning. The final letter of the Tetragrammaton, *Hei* (*Malchut/Earth*/1 Percent), suddenly *returns* to the *Vav* (*Zeir Anpin*/99 Percent) and reconnects with it, for they are no longer dissimilar. Spiritual energy is now free to flow to us once again. The Name of God (true reality) is now unified with respect to this one particular area of our lives.

REPENTANCE

Return the HEI to the VAV

Past Lives

Suppose for a moment that there is severe chaos in our lives right now, and it's *not* a result of something we did in this lifetime. Suppose instead that this chaos is caused by something we did in a *previous* lifetime. How do we *return* that far back in time? First you should know that the Adversary will try to convince you that there is no such thing as reincarnation. He will flood your mind with all sorts of obstacles so that you cannot feel the truth of previous incarnations. Also, he will summon forth feelings of self-pity and victimization that will cause you to blame everyone else for all the chaos in your life.

The way out of this hopeless mess is *to return*. The moment you stop being a victim and stop believing that you're blameless for all your suffering, you will, for all intents and purposes, return to a previous lifetime, on a soul level.

Follow this next idea carefully: acknowledging that you are responsible will be painful. It hurts. That particular pain, along with the chaos you are experiencing right now, is the exact same pain that you caused someone in a previous life. So your time-travel machine consists of accountability, responsibility, and the pain associated with letting go of being a helpless victim. If you embrace the pain and use the tools of Kabbalah to try to change your ways, you will return the *Hei* to the *Vav* and unify the 1 percent with the 99 Percent.

This time travel and the change are undetectable to your physical senses. But they are real; more real than anything else you have ever experienced.

Essentially, you have two choices in life: Accept the chaos and pain currently afflicting you and use it to transform yourself— or reject this whole idea and continue living the way everyone else has for the last few thousand years. Accepting all the existing chaos in your life and using it as an opportunity to cleanse yourself of self-interest is the only way to return in time to the time of your misdeeds, so that you can restore balance to the universe and return our universe to the World of Light, the glorious 99 Percent Reality.

Armed with these Kabbalistic insights into life, we can now understand why all chaos and pain arise in the first place. They present us with an opportunity to repent (there's that dangerous word again). It's an opportunity to *return* to the scenes of our crimes—those committed in this life, and those committed in past lives—and to repay some karmic debt. The more karmic debt we repay, the happier we become.

When you accept the pain, when you welcome the chaos, you return your soul—and a portion of this world—to the World of Light. But if you fight the pain, if you let yourself become consumed with self-pity and the old "Why me?" victim state of consciousness, not only do you forsake an opportunity to lessen your chaos and return your life to the Light but you create even more space, more distance, more separation between yourself and the Light of the Creator. the *Hei* moves farther away from the Vav.

This secret of the *Zohar* also helps us understand an even greater secret relating to Christianity and the concept of the Son of God, repentance, and the Redemption of the world, which are in fact, Kabbalistic. The *Zohar* explains that the *Vav* is known as *The Son*, and the *Yud* is called *The Father*. In regards to the son and the concept of repentance, the *Zohar* states in *Naso*, Vol. 17:

> *"For those who repent, they return the letter Hei to the letter Vav which is the son of Yud and Hei. Thus, through him Yud, Hei, Vav, Hei (the four-letter Name of God) is completed, because the son is the secret of Vav."*

> *"...When a person sins, he certainly causes the Hei to distance itself from the Vav, since the son of Yud-Hei removes itself from the Hei. ...Whoever repents affects the return of the Hei to the letter Vav, and redemption depends upon it. Consequently, everything depends on repentance."*

Repentance is all about connecting to *The Son* (*Vav*), which is just a code word for *Zeir Anpin*, the 99 Percent Realm. We do that by imitating the nature and behavior of the Light, which is unconditional sharing. Repentance is all about becoming accountable for our own negative actions and removing the traits that prevent us from emulating the Light. When we do become accountable and change our negative traits, we reconnect to the dimension called *The Son*, which in turn, allows us to connect to the highest letter of the Tetragrammaton, *Yud*, which the *Zohar* designates as *Chochmah* and *Supernal Aba* (the Father).

4-LETTER NAME OF GOD

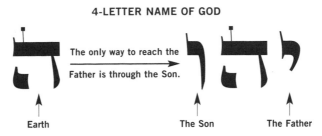

The only way to reach the Father is through the Son.

Earth   The Son   The Father

This is the secret that the great kabbalists who lived two thousand years ago tried to teach the world. Rav Akiva, Rav Joshua ben Joseph (Jesus), and of course Rav Shimon bar Yochai all tried to teach the world the true meaning and power of repentance and returning. Only the kabbalists possessed this knowledge, and this is why the *Zohar* refers to all kabbalists as "the Son of the Holy One, blessed be He."

This next excerpt from the *Zohar* gives us the path to our Final Redemption and the end of death. The *Zohar* says the distance between the *Hei* and the *Vav*, the space between the 1 Percent and the 99 Percent, is the reason the Second Temple was laid to waste in Jerusalem two thousand years ago. The reason for the distance between these two realms was that the Israelites refused to *repent*, which means they refused to transform their nonstop receiving behavior into unconditional acts of sharing. Because of this refusal to change, the Temple was destroyed. We have spent the last two thousand years trying to repair the damage that was done in Jerusalem, the world, and the cosmos so long ago. Yet the secrets of Kabbalah were hidden from the masses, so no one knew the way back home. But now we do. For the first time in human history, the *Zohar* is now available to anyone, anywhere in the world, which leads us to the most important question in this book:

How do we finally repair the world and *return* human existence to a state of immortality and never-ending happiness?

Says the Zohar: *"The reckoned days of the coming of Messiah have passed . . . and it is now contingent upon repentance only, which is the completion of His Name, which is the secret meaning of Hei that completes his name when added to Yud-Hei-Vav."*

The *Zohar* is telling us that the opportunity for the Messiah to come and redeem us has passed. We blew it on Mount Sinai with Moses, and we blew it two thousand years ago when the kabbalists tried to share the wisdom of Kabbalah with people who were just not ready to accept responsibility. Now is up to the people of the world, every one of us, to make a personal transformation through the power of repentance, which simply entails accountability and the willingness to change from being receivers into being sharers.

This task is less daunting than it might appear. In fact, it's remarkably simple. We must incorporate small actions of sharing into our lives each day. We should also try to accept any pain we feel and use it as a cleansing agent. We should resist, even if only a little bit, the desire to blame others, even when it seems justified or understandable. As best as we can, we should practice using a few of these tools each day. Start with baby steps. One day at a time. Before you know it, the world around you will start to change.

But don't believe me. Try it out. The proof must always, *always* be in the pudding.

97 Percent and 3 Percent

The kabbalistic approach to ending death in this world—because that is the only purpose of this path and the only reason to walk it—is to get 3 percent of the world to practice 97 percent of the tools presented in this book, and to get 97 percent of the world to practice just 3 percent of the tools in this book. From the combined efforts of the 3 percent and the 97 percent who are walking in the way of the kabbalist something spectacular and unimaginable will take place on Earth. The same way the Berlin Wall fell down peacefully and the Soviet Union crumbled without the need of bloodshed, all the wars, conflicts, and evils of this world will literally crumble before our eyes—mercifully, and peacefully. Death will disappear in a way we cannot imagine right now. But it will happen. And when it does, when the tears stop flowing forever, it will all seem perfectly normal, as natural as our cozy bed feels when we wake from a scary dream.

You now have this power in the palms of your hands.

Always respect it.

Constantly share it.

More From Bestselling Author Yehuda Berg

The Power of Kabbalah

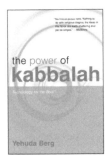

Imagine your life filled with unending joy, purpose, and contentment. Imagine your days infused with pure insight and energy. This is *The Power of Kabbalah*. It is the path from the momentary pleasure that most of us settle for, to the lasting fulfillment that is yours to claim. Your deepest desires are waiting to be realized. Find out how, in this basic introduction to the ancient wisdom of Kabbalah.

The 72 Names of God: Technology for the Soul™

The 72 Names of God are not "names" in any ordinary sense, but a state-of-the-art technology that deeply touches the human soul and is the key to ridding yourself of depression, stress, stagnation, anger, and many other emotional and physical problems. The Names represent a connection to the infinite spiritual current that flows through the universe. When you correctly bring these power sources together, you are able to gain control over your life and transform it for the better.

The Prayer of the Kabbalist: The 42 - Letter Name of God

According to the ancient wisdom of Kabbalah, the powerful prayer known as *Ana Bekho'ah* invokes The 42-Letter Name of God, which connects to no less than the undiluted force of creation. By tapping into this connection through the Prayer, you can leave the past behind and make a fresh start. If you recite the Prayer on a regular basis, you are able to use the force of creation to create miracles, both in your everyday life and in the world at large. This book explains the meaning behind the 42 letters and gives you practical steps for how best to connect to their power.

Angel Intelligence

Discover how billions of angels exist and shape the world, and how, through your thoughts and deeds, you have the power to create them, whether positive or negative. You'll learn their individual names and characteristics and their unique roles, as well as how to call on them for different purposes and use them as powerful spiritual tools for transformation. By becoming aware of the angel dynamics at work in the universe and by learning how to connect with these unseen energy forces, you will gain amazing insight and the ability to meet life's greatest challenges.

Kabbalah on the Sabbath

According to Kabbalah, the period between Friday sunset and Saturday sunset is very different from, and more important than, any of the other days of the week. Kabbalists believe that the Sabbath is the only day when the spiritual and physical worlds are united, making it the most powerful day. The Light force flows continually, giving the opportunity to refuel energy and rejuvenate the soul for the coming week. But, the day is not one of rest, nor is it about worship; it's about making a connection, which takes spiritual work. This book clearly explains how to make that connection.

The Red String Book: The Power of Protection

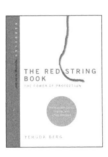

Discover the ancient wisdom behind the popularity of the Red String—the timeless technology known as Kabbalah. Worn on the left wrist, an authentic Red String provides protection against the "Evil Eye"—all negative effects that exist in the world. In *The Red String Book*, Yehuda Berg reveals how everyone can learn to use this simple yet effective tool for self-defense and healing.

The Spiritual Rules of Engagement

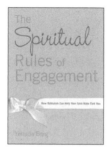

If you've been searching for your soul mate without success, maybe it's time to try a new approach: *The Spiritual Rules of Engagement*. Kabbalah teaches that we are not alone, and that we are destined to be happy. Find out how the Laws of the Universe work in your favor, once you begin to understand them and recognize the full potential for true love and sharing that lies within all of us. If you are willing to make the spiritual effort, you will see that real connection, both with the Light and with another human being, comes down to a matter of consciousness and certainty. The power is in your hands.

The Kabbalah Book of Sex: & Other Mysteries of the Universe

According to Kabbalah, the key to fulfilling sex lies in self awareness, not simply technique. Sex is the most powerful way to experience the Light of the Creator, and one of the most powerful ways to transform the world. *The Kabbalah Book of Sex* provides a solid foundation for understanding the origins of sex and its purpose, as well as practical kabbalistic tools to ignite your sex life. This groundbreaking guide teaches how to access higher levels of connection—to ourselves, our partners, and to spirit—and achieve unending passion, profound pleasure, and true fulfillment.

Living Kabbalah: A Practical System for Making the Power Work for You

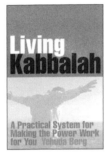

Living Kabbalah is a unique system of technology meant for you to use to transform your life and achieve true and lasting fulfillment. In these pages, you will find practical tools and exercises to help you break negative patterns, overcome challenges, and incorporate the time-tested wisdom of Kabbalah into your daily life. Noted author and teacher Yehuda Berg provides a clear blueprint that guides you step-by-step along the path toward the ultimate attainment of all that you need and desire.

Tap into a greater power—the power of Kabbalah—and learn to live more fully, richly, and joyfully every day, starting today!

The Living Kabbalah System™: Levels 1, 2 & 3

Take Your Life to the Next Level™ with this step-by-step, 23-day system for transforming your life and achieving lasting fulfillment.

Created by Yehuda Berg and based on his belief that Kabbalah should be lived, not merely studied, this revolutionary interactive system incorporates the latest learning strategies, addressing all three learning styles:

- Auditory (recorded audio sessions)

- Visual (workbook with written concepts and graphics)

- Tactile (written exercises, self-assessments, and physical tools)

The sturdy carrying case makes the system easy and convenient to use, in the car, at the gym, on a plane, wherever and whenever you choose. Learn from today's great Kabbalah leaders in an intimate, one-on-one learning atmosphere. You get practical, actionable tools and exercises to integrate the wisdom of Kabbalah into your daily life. In just 23 days you can learn to live with greater intensity, be more successful in business and relationships, and achieve your dreams. Why wait? Take your life to the next level starting today.

More Books That Can Help You Bring the Wisdom of Kabbalah into your Life

Days of Connection
By Michael Berg

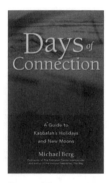

The ancient wisdom of Kabbalah teaches that each month of the lunar year holds different opportunities for us to grow and change and, conversely, holds unique pitfalls for getting stalled on our journey toward spiritual transformation. The special power of each month is strongest at its beginning, the time of the new moon, known as Rosh Chodesh. And holidays are unmatched as windows in time that make specific kinds of spiritual energy available to us. In *Days of Connection*, Michael Berg guides us through the kabbalistic calendar and explains the meaning and power behind all of these special days.

Well of Life: Kabbalistic Wisdom from a Depth of Knowledge
By Michael Berg

Kabbalah teaches that portions of the Bible connect to distinct weekly energies, and tapping into those energies helps to connect us with the Light. Here, in 52 short chapters, corresponding to each week of the lunar year, Michael Berg decodes key stories from the Bible, revealing the lessons to be learned from them, and shows you how you can maximize each week's energy to create a more meaningful life.

Secrets of the Zohar: Stories and Meditations to Awaken the Heart
By Michael Berg

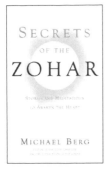

The *Zohar*'s secrets are the secrets of the Bible, passed on as oral tradition and then recorded as a sacred text that remained hidden for thousands of years. They have never been revealed quite as they are here in these pages, which decipher the codes behind the best stories of the ancient sages and offer a special meditation for each one. Entire portions of the *Zohar* are presented, with the Aramaic and its English translation in side-by-side columns. This allows you to scan and to read aloud so that you can draw on the *Zohar*'s full energy and achieve spiritual transformation. Open this book and open your heart to the Light of the *Zohar*!

Immortality: The Inevitability of Eternal Life
By Rav Berg

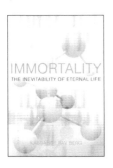

This book will totally change the way in which you perceive the world, if you simply approach its contents with an open mind and an open heart.

Most people have it backwards, dreading and battling what they see as the inevitability of aging and death. But, according to the great Kabbalist Rav Berg and the ancient wisdom of Kabbalah, it is eternal life that is inevitable.

With a radical shift in our cosmic awareness and the transformation of the collective consciousness that will follow, we can bring about the demise of the death force once and for all—in this "lifetime."

Kabbalistic Astrology: And the Meaning of Our Lives
By Rav Berg

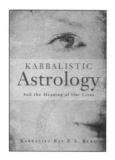

Discover your true nature and destiny, and how to shape it, through the power of Kabbalistic astrology.

Much more than a book of horoscopes, *Kabbalistic Astrology* is a tool for understanding one's individual nature at its deepest level and putting that knowledge to immediate use in the real world. It explains why destiny is not the same as predestination; it teaches that we have many possible futures and can become masters of our fate.

God Wears Lipstick: Kabbalah for Women
By Karen Berg

For thousands of years, women were banned from studying Kabbalah, the ancient source of wisdom that explains who we are and what our purpose is in this universe. Karen Berg changed that. She opened the doors of The Kabbalah Centre to all who would seek to learn.

In God Wears Lipstick, Karen Berg shares the wisdom of Kabbalah, especially as it affects you and your relationships. She reveals a woman's special place in the universe and why women have a spiritual advantage over men. She explains how to find your soulmate and your purpose in life, and empowers you to become a better human being.

The Zohar

Composed more than 2,000 years ago, the *Zohar* is a set of 23 books, a commentary on biblical and spiritual matters in the form of conversations among spiritual masters. But to describe the *Zohar* only in physical terms is greatly misleading. In truth, the *Zohar* is nothing less than a powerful tool for achieving the most important purposes of our lives. It was given to all humankind by the Creator to bring us protection, to connect us with the Creator's Light, and ultimately to fulfill our birthright of true spiritual transformation.

More than eighty years ago, when The Kabbalah Centre was founded, the *Zohar* had virtually disappeared from the world. Few people in the general population had ever heard of it. Whoever sought to read it—in any country, in any language, at any price—faced a long and futile search.

Today all this has changed. Through the work of The Kabbalah Centre and the editorial efforts of Michael Berg, the *Zohar* is now being brought to the world, not only in the original Aramaic language but also in English. The new English *Zohar* provides everything for connecting to this sacred text on all levels: the original Aramaic text for scanning; an English translation; and clear, concise commentary for study and learning.

The Kabbalah Centre®

The Kabbalah Centre® is a spiritual organization dedicated to bringing the wisdom of Kabbalah to the world. The Kabbalah Centre® itself
has existed for more than 80 years, but its spiritual lineage extends
back to Rav Isaac Luria in the 16th century and even further back
to Rav Shimon bar Yochai, who revealed the principal text of
Kabbalah, the Zohar, more than 2,000 years ago.

The Kabbalah Centre® was founded in 1922 by Rav Yehuda Ashlag,
one of the greatest kabbalists of the 20th Century. When Rav Ashlag
left this world, leadership of The Kabbalah Centre® was taken on by
Rav Yehuda Brandwein. Before his passing, Rav Brandwein designated Rav Berg as director of The Kabbalah Centre®. Now, for more
than 30 years, The Kabbalah Centre® has been under the direction
of Rav Berg, his wife Karen Berg, and their sons, Yehuda Berg and
Michael Berg.

Although there are many scholarly studies of Kabbalah, The
Kabbalah Centre® does not teach Kabbalah as an academic discipline but as a way of creating a better life. The mission of The
Kabbalah Centre® is to make the practical tools and spiritual teachings of Kabbalah available and accessible to everyone regardless of
religion, ethnicity, gender or age.

The Kabbalah Centre® makes no promises. But if people are willing
to work hard to grow and become actively sharing, caring and toler-
ant human beings, Kabbalah teaches that they will then experience
fulfillment and joy in a way previously unknown to them. This sense
of fulfillment, however, comes gradually and is always the result of
the student's spiritual work.

Our ultimate goal is for all humanity to gain the happiness and ful-fillment that is our true destiny.

Kabbalah teaches its students to question and test everything they learn. One of the most important teachings of Kabbalah is that there is no coercion in spirituality.

What Does The Kabbalah Centre® Offer?

Local Kabbalah Centres around the world offer onsite lectures, class-es, study groups, holiday celebrations and services, and a commu-nity of teachers and fellow students. To find a Centre near you, go to www.kabbalah.com.

For those of you unable to access a physical Kabbalah Centre due to the constraints of location or time, we have other ways to partici-pate in The Kabbalah Centre® community.

At www.kabbalah.com, we feature online blogs, newsletters, weekly wisdom, a store, and much more.

It's a wonderful way to stay tuned in and in touch, and it gives you access to programs that will expand your mind and challenge you to continue your spiritual work.

Student Support

The Kabbalah Centre® empowers people to take responsibility for their own lives. It's about the teachings, not the teachers. But on your journey to personal growth, things can be unclear and some-times rocky, so it is helpful to have a coach or teacher. Simply call 1 800 KABBALAH toll free.

All Student Support instructors have studied Kabbalah under the direct supervision of Kabbalist Rav Berg, widely recognized as the preeminent kabbalist of our time.

We have also created opportunities for you to interact with other Student Support students through study groups, monthly connections, holiday retreats, and other events held around the country.

I extend the greatest love to my husband, James, and to our children, Jody, Marc, Tamara, Judine and James. Our connection has and continues to be one of the greatest lights on my spiritual path. Many thanks to all responsible for bringing this awesome book to the world. Love your neighbor as yourself.

Donna